GW01465039

T

The Gospel
of Matthew

Translated by
Kalmia Bittleston

Floris Books

First published by Floris Books in 1988

British Library CIP data available

ISBN 0-86315-070-5

Printed in Great Britain
at the University Printing House, Oxford

Contents

The birth, Baptism, and Temptation

The Sermon on the Mount

Healings in Galilee

Teachings for the disciples

The rejection of John the Baptist and of Jesus

Parables and teachings of the kingdom of the heavens

The Feedings and the Transfiguration

Discourse on childhood and forgiveness

The journey to Jerusalem

Discourse on entering the kingdom of the heavens

The Passion, death and Resurrection

Introduction

Adam Bittleston

The writers of all four Gospels had a devoted, living knowledge of the Old Testament. It was present in their souls like the breath in their bodies. In everything they wrote, its words echoed. This is most clearly evident in the Gospel of St Matthew — and sometimes in ways that a reader in the present time can find disconcerting. From the first chapter onwards, passages from the Old Testament are directly quoted; and it is said that events in the life of Jesus fulfilled what these passages prophesied, even that these events happened in order to fulfil them. The present-day reader may know that the learning of the last two centuries has often interpreted these passages in the Old Testament quite differently, as referring to events in the history of Israel much nearer to the time of the original writers. Even if he does not, he may feel that St Matthew is straining the interpretation of such passages to make them fit. And in other ways too, the present-day reader may feel that while all the Evangelists are at home in the history of Israel, St Matthew is almost its prisoner. Is he writing only for the Jews, to the Jews?

They are indeed intensely concerned with their own

destiny as a people. But there is always an underlying theme in the writings, the Psalms, and the prophets: what the people of Israel suffer and achieve is not only for themselves, but it is significant for all mankind; it is a kind of parable of what every human being endures on the path towards spiritual maturity. A parable can be interpreted on many different levels, and has many applications to events in the course of history. The Old Testament is not simply a chronicle of events; its greatest figures — Moses, David, the prophets — are inspired with a poetry reaching far beyond the circumstances of their own lives and times. Such poetry is written down — but the written words are like a tomb, unless their meaning reawakens in living hearts.

St Matthew's Gospel distinguishes very clearly three ways of receiving inspired words. The 'scribes and Pharisees' take them only as if they were statements about the physical world and explicit rules of conduct. For 'the crowds' they live indeed in the heart, but like a shared dream to waken and be interpreted only at a later time. But there are some who have begun what is often a lonely struggle to understand the world and themselves; and they want to grasp what they hear with their whole being — with questioning minds, warm hearts, and strong wills. The Apostles are human individualities of this kind.

The distinction between these three groups is one of the themes which Matthew has woven into the whole composition of his Gospel, which contains five discourses, beginning with the Sermon on the Mount (Chapters 5–7) and ending with a great discourse about the future of the world (Chapters 23–25 or 24–25). Careful distinctions are made about the hearers of these discourses, and some indications are given of where they were spoken which can be supplemented by ancient traditions.

Before the Sermon on the Mount, some of the Apostles have been named, and have been told what their task is to be: 'I will make you fishers of men.' And the kinds of people are described, who come in crowds to Jesus; the many illnesses, the many regions of Israel, which are represented among them. But when Jesus, having ascended the mountain, begins to speak, it is in the first place to the disciples. 'There he sat down, and his disciples came to him. Then opening his mouth he taught them, and said . . .'

Much in the Sermon on the Mount can come nearer to the reader, if he remembers that it is spoken primarily to people who are already committed to the chief task of their lives, and is about the consequences of this commitment. Yet the fact that he speaks to the disciples in this way has a great impact on the crowds as well, as is described at the end; it is something utterly different from the way of speaking practised by the Scribes.

The second discourse (10:5–42) is quite specifically directed towards the twelve Apostles, who have all just been named; they are sent out to all the regions of Israel, and told how they are to bear themselves, both when they are accepted and when they are rejected.

The third (Chapter 13) begins with teaching given to the crowds, with Jesus sitting in a boat on the lake and the crowds standing on the shore. Later (13:36) Jesus 'sent away the crowds and went into the house.' The whole discourse is concerned with parables and their interpretation. The crowds listen to the parables, but do not understand them, though they make a deep

13

impression — rather as a dream can be impressive, without being interpreted. But the disciples are to understand — and are given some special parables, not given to the crowds.

Between the third and fourth discourses there are several very significant events, through which the disciples can learn more intimately about the quality of their own community; among them the Feeding of the Five Thousand, and the Transfiguration. In the last only Peter, James and John share, from among the twelve. It is again a mountain; traditionally Mount Tabor, no longer looking over the lake, but a mountain among mountains. The minds of the disciples are now directed more explicitly to the Passion and Resurrection.

Chapter 18 is about childhood and forgiveness, closely connected themes; for children forgive most thoroughly, both adults and each other.

After this discourse, Jesus leaves Galilee. All that follows is set in the stern environment of Judea and the desert beyond the Jordan. And here Matthew's narrative joins, in its sequence of events, the other three Evangelists, particularly during the last week leading up to Easter Day. During this week comes the 'little Apocalypse', the description of the future of the world, which is found in Mark and Luke, but not in John. In Matthew this is part of the last, the fifth discourse. It is not unmistakably clear where this begins. If we reckon in the 'Woes' as balancing the eight Beatitudes, it can be regarded as beginning with Chapter 23, 'Then Jesus spoke to the crowds and his disciples . . .', and as spoken in the Temple at Jerusalem; Chapter 24, says 'Jesus went out of the Temple . . .' And there follows the enigmatic indication that at this moment the disciples came to *show* him the buildings of the Temple. Were these not very familiar to him from years past?

St John's Gospel bears witness that at a much earlier time Jesus had said 'Destroy this Temple, and I will build it up in three days.' The false witness reported by St Matthew at the trial before Caiaphas seems to refer to this saying, which St John makes clear referred to Christ's own body. This helps with all the references to the Temple and indeed to the 'house' in the Gospels. What man builds on earth, whether as dwelling-place for the divine or for his own kind, is always an image and parable of the physical body, fashioned in God's likeness. And if the true Spirit no longer indwells it, it is left 'forsaken and desolate', as Jerusalem is, in spite of the vast crowds moving through its narrow streets. From among these crowds many people can be found prepared to join in the cries of hatred and condemnation against Jesus, which go with him until his death upon the cross. Very few among those who had followed him during the years of his ministry, and had heard his teaching, are able to stand near him underneath the cross, and accompany his body to the grave. And at first it is very few who are able to look at Easter on the new body, the Temple built afresh, in which Christ's Spirit dwells from then onwards.

In the accounts given by the four Evangelists of the events following the Resurrection there are many differences of detail, though the substantial fact is the same. Matthew alone describes two scenes which form a deeply moving contrast. In the first, the soldiers who have been set to guard the tomb see the angel who has rolled back the stone from the entrance to the sepulchre; 'And from fear of him the guards were shaken and became as if they were dead' (28:4). Some of the guards go to the chief priests and tell what has happened; and are bribed to say that disciples of Jesus came while the guards were sleeping and stole away his body. And thus this lie becomes widespread in the years that follow. The second scene, with which the Gospel of St Matthew ends, is a meeting of the Risen Christ with the Apostles, not described in the other Gospels, upon a mountain in Galilee. Here they are entrusted with great, living truths, which are to spread through all humanity over millennia.

> Go therefore
> And make disciples of all the nations
> Baptizing them
> In the name of the Father
> And of the Son
> And of the Holy Spirit
>
> Teaching them to obey everything
> That I have commanded you
> And how
> I
> I am with you
> Every day
> Until the ending of the age

Translator's note

The first aim of any translation of the Gospels must
be transparency, because behind the record of Christ's
teaching and of his deeds, which is given by the Evangelists, stands the reality of his life on earth. Their account
was first incarnated into the Greek language, but now
exists in hundreds of different languages and even
dialects. The layout of this translation, which may at
first suggest verse, is also in support of clarity. The
narrative has been separated from direct speech; whether
it is Jesus himself speaking, or one of his disciples, or
perhaps another actor in the drama. The Gospels are
indeed dramatic, and because the short lines of this
translation carry the reader forward, it should be read
slowly, no faster than reading aloud. In the early Chris-
tian centuries, congregations gathered together to hear
the Gospel read. Very few would have been able to own
a copy of even part of one of the Gospels. They were
intended to be heard, and have the rhythms and
repetitions of speech, so that they can be remembered.

It is important to think over the Gospel, and to get
away from the printed page, so that the words live as if
heard in an inner world; although experience shows
how difficult it is to recall *exactly* what has been read.
All translators will feel that every word counts, but

17

words are so alive that in another setting the meaning can be different, and all attempts always to translate the same Greek word by the same word in English have run into difficulties.

On the other hand, there are important Greek words which are often repeated, then it may be possible to come to a decision and try to be consistent, so that such words or phrases recur like a theme in music. Not only do words live, but language as a whole is always changing, and the Gospels are there for the people of the present time. This can be the only justification for a fresh attempt at a task at which so many have laboured with the whole of their hearts.

Kalmia Bittleston

1 *The genealogy*

1   The record of the genesis
    Of Jesus Christ
    The son of David
    The son of Abraham

2   Abraham was the father of Isaac
    And Isaac of Jacob
    And Jacob of Judah and his brothers

3   Judah was the father of Perez
    And of Zerah
    Their mother was Tamar

    Perez was the father of Hezron
    And Hezron of Ram
4   And Ram of Amminadab
    And Amminadab of Nahshon
    And Nahshon of Salmon

5   Salmon was the father of Boaz
    Whose mother was Rahab
    And Boaz was the father of Obed
    Whose mother was Ruth

6   And Obed was the father of Jesse
    Who was the father of David the King

    David was the father of Solomon
    Whose mother had been the wife of Uriah

7   Solomon was the father of Rehoboam
And Rehoboam of Abijah
And Abijah of Asa

8   Asa was the father of Jehoshaphat
And Jehoshaphat of Joram
And Joram of Uzziah

9   Uzziah was the father of Jotham
And Jotham of Ahaz
And Ahaz of Hezekiah

10   Hezekiah was the father of Manasseh
And Manasseh of Amos
And Amos of Josiah
11   And Josiah of Jechoniah and his brothers
At the deportation to Babylon

12   After the deportation to Babylon
Jechoniah was the father of Shealtiel
And Shealtiel of Zerubbabel
13   And Zerubbabel of Abiud
And Abiud of Eliakim
And Eliakim of Azor

14   Azor was the father of Zadok
And Zadok of Achim
And Achim of Eliud
15   And Eliud of Eleazar
And Eleazar of Matthan
And Matthan of Jacob

16   Jacob was the father of Joseph
     The husband of Mary
     Of whom was born Jesus
     Who is called Christ

17   Therefore all the generations
     From Abraham to David
     Were fourteen generations
     And from David
     Until the deportation to Babylon
     Were fourteen generations
     And from the deportation to Babylon
     Until the Christ
     Were fourteen generations

The birth of Jesus Christ

18   Now the birth of Jesus Christ
     Happened in this way

     His mother Mary
     Was promised in marriage to Joseph
     But before they came together
     She was found to have conceived
     By the Holy Spirit

19   As her husband Joseph
     Was an upright man
     And did not wish
     To make an example of her
     He resolved to dismiss her secretly

20 But while he was thinking of this
An angel of the Lord
Appeared to him in a dream
    And said
        Joseph son of David
        Do not be afraid
        To take your wife Mary
        As her conception
        Is of the Holy Spirit

21   She will give birth to a son
        And you shall give him
        The name Jesus
        Because he will save his people
        From their sins

22 All this happened
So that might be fulfilled
What was spoken by the Lord
Through the prophet
Saying
23 *Now the Virgin will conceive*
And will give birth to a son
And they will call his name
Emmanuel
Which is translated
God with us

24   When Joseph rose up from sleep
He did what the angel of the Lord
Had commanded him
And took his wife

25   He did not know her
Until she had borne a son
And he gave him
The name Jesus

2   *The visit of the Magi*

1   Now when Jesus was born
In Bethlehem of Judea
During the reign of King Herod
Magi from the East
Arrived in Jerusalem

2   And they said
        Where is the one
        Who is born King of the Jews?
        We have seen his star
        In the East
        And have come to worship him

3   When he heard this
King Herod was disturbed
And with him
The whole of Jerusalem

4   Having assembled
All the chief priests
And scribes of the people

He asked them
Where the Christ should be born

5   And they told him
          In Bethlehem of Judea
          As the prophet has written
6   *And you Bethlehem*
          In the land of Judah
          Are not in any way the least
          Among the leaders of Judah
          Because from you
          Will come a leader
          Who will shepherd my people Israel

7   Then Herod
Called the Magi secretly
And made careful enquiries
About the time
When the star appeared

8   He sent them to Bethlehem
          And said
               Make searching enquiries
               About the child
               And when you have found him
               Bring me the news
               So that I myself
               May also come and worship him

9   When they had heard the King
They continued on their way

And now the star
Which they saw in the East
Led them
Until it came to stand
Over where the child was

10 On seeing the star
They rejoiced with the greatest joy

11 When they came into the house
They saw the child
With his mother Mary
And they fell down
And worshipped him

They opened their treasures
And offered him gifts
Gold
Frankincense
And myrrh

12 As they had been warned
In a dream
Not to return to Herod
They took another road
And departed to their country

The flight into Egypt

13 When they had gone
An angel of the Lord
Appeared to Joseph in a dream
    And said
        Get up
        Take the child and his mother
        And go away into Egypt
        Stay there until I tell you
        As Herod
        Is now going to search for the child
        To destroy him

14 So he got up
And took the child
And his mother
At night
And went away into Egypt

15 He was there until Herod's death
To fulfil what the Lord
Had spoken through the prophet
Saying
Out of Egypt I called my son

The massacre of the innocents

16 When Herod
Saw that the Magi had scorned him
He was full of fury

26

He sent out
And killed all the boys in Bethlehem
And in the surrounding districts
Who were two years old
Or less
According to the time
Which he had carefully enquired
From the Magi

17   Then what was said
Through Jeremiah the prophet
Was fulfilled
18   *A voice was heard in Rama*
Weeping and sorrowing
Rachel weeping for her children
And would not be comforted
Because they are no more

The return from Egypt

19   When Herod had died
An angel of the Lord
Appeared in a dream
To Joseph in Egypt
20   And said
           Get up
           Take the child and his mother
           And go into the land of Israel
           Because the people are dead
           Who wished to take the child's life

21 So he got up
And taking the child
And his mother
He went into the land of Israel

22 But when he heard that Archelaus
Was ruling over Judea
In place of his father Herod
He was afraid to go there

And being warned in a dream
He turned away
Into the region of Galilee
23 And went to live
In a town called Nazareth
So that what was spoken
Through the prophets
Was fulfilled
He shall be called a Nazarene

3 *The preaching of John the Baptist*
1 Now in those days
John the Baptist appeared
Preaching in the desert of Judea
2   And saying
                Change your hearts and minds
                As the kingdom of the heavens
                Has come close

3   This is the one
        Who is spoken of
        Through Isaiah the prophet
        When he says
        A voice is calling in the desert
        Prepare the road for the Lord
        Make his paths straight

4   John himself
        Wore a garment of camel hair
        With a leather belt round his waist
        His food was locusts and wild honey

5   Then all Jerusalem
        Went out to him
        And all Judea
        And all the neighbourhood
        Of the Jordan

6   And they were baptized
        In the River Jordan
        Acknowledging their sins

7   When he saw many of the Pharisees
        And Sadducees
        Coming to the baptism
            He said to them
                Offspring of vipers
                Who warned you to escape
                From the anger which is to come?

8   Therefore bear fruit
    Worthy of your change of heart
9   And do not think to yourselves
    We have Abraham as our father
    Because I say to you
    That from these stones
    God has the power
    To raise up children to Abraham

10 The axe is already laid
    At the root of the trees
    Therefore every tree
    That does not bear sound fruit
    Is cut down
    And thrown into the fire

11 I myself
    Baptize you in water
    For a change of heart and mind
    But the one
    Who comes after me
    Who is stronger than I am
    And of whom I am not worthy
    To carry the sandals
    He will baptize you
    In Holy Spirit and fire

12 The winnowing fan
    Is in his hand
    And he will sweep clean
    His threshing floor

He will gather the wheat
Into the barn
But the chaff
He will burn with a fire
That cannot be put out

Jesus is baptized

13 Then Jesus appeared from Galilee
Coming to John at the Jordan
To be baptized by him

14 But John
Was determined to prevent it
Saying to him
I myself
Need to be baptized by you
And yet you come to me?

15 Jesus answered him
Allow it now
As it is proper for us
To complete all that is needed

Then he allowed him

16 Jesus
Having been baptized
Came up at once
Out of the water
Then
The heavens opened

And he saw the Spirit of God
Descending like a dove
And coming down upon him

17 And now
>>A voice out of the heavens said
>>>>This is my son
>>>>My beloved
>>>>In whom I rejoice

4 *The Temptation*

1 Then Jesus
Was led by the Spirit
Into the desert
To be tempted by the devil

2 He fasted forty days
And forty nights
And afterwards he was hungry

And approaching

3 Then the tempter came to him
>>And said *to him :*
>>>>If you are God's son
>>>>*Tell* Speak to these stones
>>>>That they may become
>>>>Loaves of bread

4 But he answered him
>>It has been written
>>>>*Mankind*
>>>>*Shall not only live on bread* *alone*

32

> *But on every word*
> *That comes from the mouth of God*

5 Then the devil
Takes Took him into the holy city
And stood him
On the parapet of the Temple
6 *says* And said to him
> If you are God's son
> Throw yourself down

For As it has been written
> *He will command his angels*
> *To be concerned with you*
> *And on their hands*
> *They will carry you*
> *Lest you strike your foot*
> *Against a stone*

7 Jesus said to him
> Again it has been written
> *You shall not*
> *Put the Lord your God*
> *To the test*

8 Again the devil
Takes Took him to a very high mountain
shows And showed him
All the kingdoms of the world
And their magnificence
9 And said to him

33

I will give all this *these*
To you
If you will fall down
And worship me

10   Then Jesus *says* said to him
          Go
          Satan
   For   As it has been written
          You shall worship
          The Lord your God
          And you shall serve him only

11   Then the devil left him *leaves*
     And *behind* now angels
     Came to bring him aid
   Approached and ministered to him

Jesus returns to Galilee

12   When he heard
     That John had been arrested
     He went away into Galilee

13   He left Nazareth
     And came to live in Capernaum
     By the sea
     In the district of Zebulun and Naphtali

14   So that what was said
     Through Isaiah the prophet
     Might be fulfilled

15   *Land of Zebulun*

And land of Naphtali
The sea road
Beyond the Jordan
Galilee of the Gentiles

16 *The people who dwelt in darkness*
Have seen a great light
And for those
Who dwelt in the region
And shadow of death
Light has dawned

17 From then on
Jesus began to preach
    And said
        Change your hearts and minds
        As the kingdom of the heavens
        Has come close

The calling of four disciples
18 As he walked
Beside the Sea of Galilee
He saw two brothers
Simon called Peter
And his brother Andrew
Casting a net into the sea
Because they were fishers
19   And he said to them
        Come with me
        And I will make you
        Fishers of men

20 Immediately
They left their nets
And followed him

21 Going farther on
He saw two other brothers
James the son of Zebedee
And his brother John
In the boat
With Zebedee their father
Mending their nets

He called them
22 Then at once
They left the boat
And their father
And followed him

Jesus preaches and heals in Galilee
23 He went round
The whole of Galilee
Teaching in their synagogues
Preaching the Gospel of the kingdom
And healing all diseases
And all disabilities
Among the people

24 News of him
Spread into the whole of Syria
And they brought to him all those
Who were suffering from various diseases

Or were in pain
Also those who were possessed by demons
Or were lunatics
Or paralysed
And he healed them

25 Large crowds followed him
From Galilee
And the Decapolis
And Jerusalem
And from Judea and beyond the Jordan

The Sermon on the Mount

5 *The Beatitudes*
1 When he saw the crowds
He went up on to the mountain
There he sat down
And his disciples came to him

2 Then opening his mouth
He taught them
    And said

3   Blessed
     Are the beggars in the spirit
     As theirs
     Is the kingdom of the heavens

4   Blessed
     Are those who mourn
     As they will be comforted

5   Blessed
     Are the gentle
     As they will inherit the earth

6   Blessed
     Are those who hunger and thirst
     For what is right
     As they will be satisfied

7   Blessed
     Are the merciful
     As they will have mercy
     Shown to them

8   Blessed
     Are those with pure hearts
     As they will see God

9   Blessed
     Are the peacemakers
     As they will be called
     Sons of God

10   Blessed
        Are those who are persecuted
        For the sake of what is right
        As theirs
        Is the kingdom of the heavens

11   Blessed
        Are you when they reproach you
        And persecute you
        For my sake
        And say many evil things
        Against you
        Which are untrue

12   Rejoice and be glad
        Because you have a great reward
        In the heavens
        As this is how they persecuted
        The prophets who came before you

Salt and light

13   You are the salt of the earth
        But how shall it be salted
        If the salt is useless?

        It is no longer worth anything
        Except to be thrown outside
        Where people will tread on it

14 You are the light of the world
A city built on a mountain
Cannot be hidden
15 Nor do people light a lamp
And put it under the corn-measure
But on the lampstand
Where it gives light
To everyone in the house

16 Let your light
Shine out to your fellow men
So that they see
The nobility of your deeds
And praise
Your Father in the heavens

The old Law and new demands
17 Do not think
That I came to destroy
The Law and the prophets
I did not come to destroy
But to complete them
18 Certainly I say to you
Until heaven and earth pass away
By no means
Will one letter
Or one comma
Pass away from the Law
Until everything has happened

19 Therefore
Whoever breaks one
Of the very least
Of these commandments
And teaches his fellow men
To do so
Will be called least
In the kingdom of the heavens
But whoever keeps
And teaches them
Will be called great
In the kingdom of the heavens

20 Because I say to you
That unless your virtue
Is more
Than that of the scribes and Pharisees
Certainly
You will not enter
The kingdom of the heavens

21 You heard
That in the past
The people were told
You shall not kill
And whoever kills
Will be judged responsible

22　　　　But I
　　　　I say to you
　　　　That everyone
　　　　Who is angry with his brother
　　　　Will be judged responsible

　　　　And whoever
　　　　Says to his brother
　　　　Worthless fellow
　　　　Must answer to the council

　　　　And whoever says
　　　　You fool
　　　　Will be in danger
　　　　Of the fire of retribution

23　　　　Therefore
　　　　If you bring your gift
　　　　To the altar of sacrifice
　　　　And then remember
　　　　That your brother
　　　　Has something against you

24　　　　Leave your gift there
　　　　In front of the altar
　　　　And first
　　　　Go and be reconciled
　　　　With your brother
　　　　And then come
　　　　And offer your gift

25 Come to terms
With your opponent
While you are with him
On the road
Or your opponent
Will hand you over
To the judge
And the judge
To the officer
And you
May be thrown into prison

26 Certainly I say to you
By no means
Will you come out of there
Until you have repaid
The last copper

27 You heard
That it was said
You shall not commit adultery

28 But I
I say to you
That everyone
Who looks at a woman
With desire
Has already committed adultery
With her
In his heart

29
So if your right eye
Causes your downfall
Pluck it out
And throw it away from you
It is to your advantage
That one of your members
Should perish
Rather
Than that your whole body
Is thrown into the fire of retribution

30
And if your right hand
Causes your downfall
Cut it off
And throw it away from you
It is to your advantage
That one of your members
Should perish
Rather
Than that your whole body
Go into the fire of retribution

31
And it was said
Whoever releases his wife
Let him give her a divorce

32
But I
I say to you
That everyone
Who releases his wife
Except for immorality

Causes her to commit adultery
And whoever
Marries a divorced woman
Commits adultery

33

Again
You heard that in the past
The people were told
You shall not swear falsely
But shall keep your vows
To the Lord

34

But I
I say to you
Do not swear at all
Either by heaven
Because it is the throne of God

35

Or by the earth
Because it is the stool
For his feet
Or by Jerusalem
Because it is the city
Of the great King

36

Or by your head
Because you cannot make one hair
White or black

37 Let your words be
Yes yes
No no
Because what is more than this
Is evil

38 You heard that it was said
An eye for an eye
And a tooth for a tooth

39 But I
I say to you
Do not oppose evil
But if anyone
Strikes you on the right cheek
Turn the other also
Towards him
And whoever

40 Would sue you
For your tunic
Allow him also
To take your cloak

41 And if anyone
Would impress you into service
To go one mile
Go with him two

42 Give to whoever asks you
And do not turn away anyone
Who wishes to borrow from you

43 You heard that it was said
You shall love your neighbour
And hate your enemy

44 But I
I say to you
Love your enemies
And pray
For those who persecute you
45 So that you may be the sons
Of your Father in the heavens
He causes his sun to rise
On those who are wicked
And on those who are good
And he sends rain
On the just and the unjust

46 If you love those who love you
What reward should you have?
Surely even the tax collectors
Do the same

47 And if you only greet your brothers
What more are you doing
Than the Gentiles
Who do the same?

48 Therefore
Become perfect
As your heavenly Father
Is perfect

6 *Almsgiving and prayer and fasting*

1   Take care
       That you do not perform
       Your virtuous deeds
       In the sight of your fellow men
       Intending them to notice you
       For then
       You will not be rewarded
       By your Father in the heavens

2   Therefore
       When you give to those in need
       Do not sound a trumpet
       In front of you
       In the synagogues
       And in the streets
       Like the hypocrites
       Who want to be praised
       By their fellow men
       Certainly I say to you
       They have their reward

3   But when you give to the needy
       Do not allow your left hand
       To be aware
       Of what your right hand does
4   So that your gift
       May be kept secret
       And your Father
       Who sees what is kept secret
       Will repay you

5
When you pray
Do not imitate the hypocrites
Because they like to pray
In the synagogues
And standing at the corners
Of the open streets
Where they are noticed
By their fellow men
Certainly I say to you
They have their reward

6
But when you pray
Go into your inner room
And when you have shut the door
Pray to your Father
Who is there in secret
And your Father
Who sees what is kept secret
Will repay you

7
In your prayers
Do not use meaningless words
Like the Gentiles
Who think
That they will be heard
Because they talk so much

8
So do not be like them
As your Father
Knows what you need
Before you ask him

9   Therefore
You should pray like this
OUR FATHER
IN THE HEAVENS
MAY YOUR NAME
BE KEPT HOLY

10   YOUR KINGDOM COME
YOUR WILL BE DONE
AS IN HEAVEN
SO ALSO ON EARTH

11   THE BREAD WE NEED EVERY DAY
GIVE US TODAY

12   AND FORGIVE US OUR DEBTS
AS WE FORGIVE OUR DEBTORS

13   DO NOT BRING US TO THE TEST
BUT RESCUE US FROM THE EVIL ONE

14   Because if you forgive
Your fellow men
Their shortcomings
Your heavenly Father
Will also forgive you

15   But if you do not forgive
Your fellow men
Neither will your Father
Forgive your shortcomings

16   When you fast
Do not appear depressed
Like the hypocrites

Because they disfigure their faces
So that their fasting
May be visible
To their fellow men
Certainly I say to you
They have their reward

17 But when you fast
Anoint your head
And wash your face
18 So that your fasting
Is not visible
To your fellow men
But to your Father
Who is there in secret
And your Father
Who sees what is kept secret
Will repay you

Serving the light
19 Do not
Store up treasure for yourselves
On the earth
Where moths and worms
Eat it away
And where thieves
Break in and steal
20 But store up treasure for yourselves
In heaven
Where neither moths nor worms

Eat it away
And where thieves
Do not break in and steal

21 Because where your treasure is
There your heart
Will be also

22 The lamp of the body
Is the eye
So if your eye sees clearly
The whole of your body
Will shine
23 But if your eye sees falsely
The whole of your body
Will be dark

If therefore
The light in you
Is darkness
How great is the darkness

24 No-one can serve two overlords
For either he will hate the one
And love the other
Or he will hold firmly to the one
And scorn the other
You are not able
To serve God and riches

Trust in God

25
　　　Therefore I say to you
　　　Do not be too concerned
　　　About your soul-bearing life
　　　About what you should eat
　　　Or what you should drink
　　　Or about your body
　　　What you should wear

　　　Is not the soul-bearing life
　　　More than food
　　　And the body
　　　More than dress?

26
　　　You should look
　　　At the birds of heaven
　　　They do not sow
　　　Neither do they reap
　　　Nor store in barns
　　　And your heavenly Father
　　　Feeds them
　　　Are you
　　　Not worth more than they are?

27
　　　But which of you
　　　By his concern
　　　Can alter the way he is made?

28
　　　And why are you concerned
　　　About dress
　　　Observe the lilies

How they grow in the fields
They do not labour or spin
29   But I say to you
That Solomon
In all his glory
Was not robed
Like one of them

30   If the grass in the fields
Which is there today
And tomorrow
Is thrown into the oven
Is so clothed by God
Will he not do much more
For you?
You that have little faith

31   Therefore do not be concerned
And say
What are we going to eat?
Or what
Are we going to drink?
Or what
Are we going to put on?

32   The Gentiles
Search for all these things
And your heavenly Father
Knows that you need them all

33 But first
Seek his kingdom
And his justice
And all these things
Will be given to you

34 Therefore do not be concerned
About tomorrow
As tomorrow
Will take care of itself
Enough for today
Are its difficulties

7 *Do not criticize others*

1 Do not judge
So that you are not judged

2 As with the judgment
With which you judge
You will be judged yourselves
And the measure
With which you measure
Will be the measure
Which is given to you

3 And why
Do you see the splinter
In your brother's eye
And do not pay attention
To the beam
In your own eye?

4
Or how will you say
To your brother
Allow me
To take the splinter
Out of your eye
When just look
What a beam
Is in your own eye?

5
Hypocrite
First take the beam
Out of your own eye
Then you will see clearly
To take the splinter
Out of your brother's eye

Giving and receiving

6
Do not give anything holy
To the dogs
Or throw down your pearls
In front of pigs
Because they may tread on them
With their feet
And then turn round
And tear you

7 Ask
And it will be given to you
Seek
And you will find
Knock
And it will be opened for you

8 As everyone who asks
Receives
And whoever seeks
Finds
And for the one who knocks
It will be opened

9 Or which man of you
When his son
Asks him for a loaf of bread
Will give him a stone?
10 Or if he asks for a fish
Will give him a snake?

11 So if you
Who are evil   *far grow good*
Know how to give good gifts
To your children
How much more
Will your Father in the heavens
Give good things
To those who ask him

12   Therefore
        Everything that you wish others
        Would do for you
        Do the same to them
        As this is the law
        And the prophets

The narrow gate

13   Go in through the narrow gate
        Because the gate is wide
        And the road is broad
        Which leads on to destruction
        And there are many *are those*
        Who enter that way

14   But because the gate is narrow
        And the road made troublesome *narrow*
        Which leads on to life
   And There are few *are those*
        Who find it

False prophets

15   Watch out for false prophets
        Who come to you
        In sheep's clothing
        But inwardly
        Are thieving wolves

16   You will recognize them
    By their fruits
    Are grapes gathered from thorns
    Or figs from thistles?

17   So every good tree
    Produces sound fruit
    But the rotten tree
    Produces evil fruit

18   A good tree
    Is not able to bear evil fruit
    Nor a rotten tree
    To bear sound fruit

19   Every tree
    That does not bear sound fruit
    Is cut down
    And thrown into the fire

20   So you will recognize them
    By their fruit

21   Not everyone who says to me
    Lord
    Lord
    Will enter
    The kingdom of the heavens
    But whoever
    Does the will of my Father
    In the heavens

22   In that day
Many will say to me
Lord
Lord
Have we not prophesied
In your name?
And cast out demons
In your name?
And done many powerful deeds
In your name?

23   Then I will declare to them
I never recognized you
Depart from me
You law-breakers

The two builders

24   So everyone who hears
These words of mine
And does them
Will be like a thoughtful man
Who built his house
On a rock

25   Then the rain poured down
The rivers rose
The winds blew
And beat upon that house
But it did not fall
Because the foundations
Were on the rock

26   But everyone who hears
      These words of mine
      And does not do them
      Will be like a foolish man
      Who built his house
      On the sand

27   Then the rain poured down
      The rivers rose
      The winds blew
      And struck against that house
      And it fell
      With a mighty fall

28 And it happened
    That when Jesus
    Had ended these words
    The crowds
    Were astonished at his teaching
29 Because he was teaching them
    As someone who had authority
    And not like their scribes

8 *A leper is cleansed*
1   As he came down from the mountain
    Large crowds followed him

2   Now a leper came to him
    And bowing down
        He said
            Lord

>   If it is your will
>   You have the power
>   To make me clean

3   He stretched out his hand
    And touched him
>   Saying
>   I will
>   You are clean

At once
He was cleared of his leprosy

4   Jesus said to him
>   See that you tell no one
>   But go
>   Show yourself to the priest
>   And offer the gift
>   Which Moses commanded
>   As evidence to the people

The healing of the centurion's servant
5   When he entered Capernaum
    A centurion came to him
    With an urgent request
6   And said
>   Sir
>   My personal attendant
>   Is lying at home
>   Paralysed and in terrible pain

7 He said to him
    I
    I will come
    And heal him

8 But the centurion said
    Sir
    I am not worthy
    To receive you under my roof
    Only speak the word
    And my attendant will be healed

9   As I myself
    Am also a man under authority
    With soldiers under me
    And I say to one
    Go
    And he goes
    And to another
    Come
    And he comes
    And to my slave
    Do this
    And he does it

10 When he heard this
Jesus was astonished
    And said to those who were following
    Certainly I say to you
    I have not found such great faith
    From any one in Israel

11   And I say to you
That many will come
From the east
And from the west
And will sit at the table
With Abraham
Isaac
And Jacob
In the kingdom of the heavens

12   But the sons of the kingdom
Will be cast out
Into the outer darkness

There will be weeping
And gnashing of teeth

13   Then Jesus said to the centurion
Go
As you believe
So may it be for you

And in that hour
The boy was healed

Jesus heals Peter's mother-in-law and many sufferers

14   Jesus went into Peter's house
And saw his mother-in-law
Laid low and suffering from fever

15   He touched her hand
The fever left her
And she got up and served them

16 When evening came
They brought to him
Many people possessed by demons
He cast out the spirits
With a word
And all who suffered
He healed

17 So that what was said
Through the prophet Isaiah
Was fulfilled
He took our disabilities
And bore our diseases

The difficulties of discipleship
18 Jesus saw that a crowd
Was gathering round him
So he gave the order to go away
To the other side

19 Then one of the scribes
Came to him and said
Teacher
I will follow you
Wherever you go

20 Jesus said to him
The foxes have holes
And the birds of heaven
Have their dwellings

But the Son of Man
Has nowhere to lay his head

21 And another of the disciples
Said to him
Lord
First let me go away
And bury my father

22 But Jesus said to him
You follow me
And leave the dead
To bury their dead

Jesus calms the storm
23 As he embarked on to the boat
His disciples followed him

24 Now a great disturbance
Took place in the sea
So that the boat
Was covered by the waves

But he was asleep
25 And they went to him
And woke him
Saying
Lord
Save us
We are lost

26   But he said to them
                Why are you such cowards
                You that have little faith?

        Then he got up
        And spoke sternly
        To the winds
        And to the sea
        And there was a great calm

27   The men were astonished
                And said
                    What sort is he
                    That even the winds
                    And the sea
                    Obey him?

Two demoniacs are healed

28   When he came to the other side
        Into the country of the Gadarenes
        Two demoniacs met him
        Coming out of the tombs

        They were exceedingly hostile
        So that no-one was strong enough
        To pass along that road

29   Now they called out
            And said
                What is there between us and you
                Son of God?

Have you come here
To torment us
Before the moment has come?

30 At a distance from them
A large herd of pigs were feeding

31 And the demons begged him
If you cast us out
Send us into the herd of pigs

32 He said to them
Go

So those who came out
Went away into the pigs

Then the whole herd
Rushed down the steep incline
Into the sea
And died in the water

33 The herdsmen fled
And went away into the town
Where they reported everything
Also what had happened to the demoniacs

34 All the townspeople came out
In order to meet Jesus
When they saw him
They begged him to leave their district

9 *A paralytic is healed*

1 Embarking on to a boat
He crossed over
And came to his home town

2 And now
They brought a paralytic to him
Lying on a mattress

When Jesus saw their faith
He said to the paralytic
Take courage
Child
Your sins are forgiven

3 Some of the scribes
Said among themselves
He blasphemes

4 As he knew their thoughts
Jesus said
Why do you think evil
In your hearts?
5 For which is easier
To say
Your sins are forgiven
Or to say
Rise up and walk?

6 Only that you may know
That the Son of Man

Has authority on the earth
To forgive sins

Then he said to the paralytic
Get up
Take your mattress
And go home

7   He got up
And went away to his house

8   But when they saw it
The people were afraid
And praised God
Who had given such authority to men

The calling of Matthew
9   He left there
And as he passed by
Jesus saw a man
Whose name was Matthew
Sitting in the custom house

He said to him
Follow me

He rose up
And followed him

10   It happened
That he was having a meal

In the house
And many tax-collectors
And outcasts
Came to sit at the table
With Jesus and his disciples

11 When they saw it
The Pharisees said to his disciples
Why does your teacher
Eat with tax-collectors
And with outcasts?

12 But when Jesus heard it
He said
Those who have good health
Do not need a doctor
But those who are suffering

13 Go and learn what that is
I wish mercy
And not sacrifice
As I did not come
To call the just
But the outcasts

A question about fasting
14 Then John's disciples
Came to him
And said
Why do we fast

And the Pharisees fast
But your disciples do not fast?

15   Jesus said to them
Can the bridegroom's attendants
    mourn
As long as the bridegroom
Is with them?
The day will come
When the bridegroom
Is taken away from them
And then they will fast

16   No one puts a patch
Of untreated cloth
On to an old cloak
As its quality
Will pull away from the cloak
And the tear
Will be made worse

17   Neither do they put new wine
Into old wineskins
Otherwise
The wineskins burst
The wine pours out
And the wineskins are destroyed

But they put new wine
Into fresh wineskins
And both are saved

The cure of a woman and the raising of a young girl

18 Now while he was still speaking
An official came up to him
And bowing down
    He said
        My daughter has just died
        But if you come
        And lay your hand on her
        She will live

19 Jesus got up
And followed him with his disciples

20 Then a woman came behind him
Who for twelve years
Had suffered from a flow of blood

She touched the fringe of his cloak
21 As she said within herself
If only
I am able to touch his cloak
I shall be saved

22 Jesus turned
And when he saw her
    He said
        Courage
        Daughter
        Your faith has healed you

And from that hour
The woman was healed

23　When Jesus came into the official's house
And saw the flute players
And the crowd
All making a noise
24　　　He said
　　　　　Leave here
　　　　　The young girl has not died
　　　　　She is asleep

But they laughed at him

25　However
When the people had been put outside
He went in
And took hold of her hand
And the young girl was raised up

26　Then this report
Went out all over the country

Two blind men are healed
27　As Jesus went on from there
Two blind men followed
　　　Calling out
　　　　　Pity us
　　　　　Son of David

28 When he entered the house
The blind men came up to him
    And Jesus said to them
        Do you believe
        That I have the power
        To do this?

    They said
        Yes
        Lord

29 Then he touched their eyes
    And said
        As is your faith
        So it shall be for you

30 Their eyes were opened
    And Jesus spoke to them sternly
    Saying
        See that no one
        Becomes aware of this

31 But they went out
And talked of him
In all the countryside

A dumb demoniac is healed

32 Just as those were leaving
They brought to him
A dumb demoniac

33 And when the demon
Was cast out
The dumb man spoke

The crowds were amazed
    And said
        Such a thing
        Has never been seen in Israel

34   But the Pharisees said
        Through the ruler of the demons
        He casts out the demons

35 Jesus went about the towns and villages
Teaching in the synagogues

Preaching the Gospel of the kingdom
And healing all diseases
And all disabilities

36 When he saw the crowds
He was full of concern for them
Because they were fainting
And scattered
Like sheep without a shepherd

37   Then he said to his disciples
        Indeed there is a great harvest
        But there are few labourers
38   Therefore pray the lord of the harvest
        To speed labourers into his harvest

10 *The sending out of the twelve*

1 He called to him
His twelve disciples
And gave them authority
Over unclean spirits
So that they could cast them out
And could heal all diseases
And all disabilities

2 These are the names
Of the twelve apostles

First Simon called Peter
And his brother Andrew
James the son of Zebedee
And his brother John
3 Philip and Bartholomew
Thomas and Matthew the tax-collector
James the son of Alphaeus
And Thaddaeus
4 Simon the Canaanaean
And Judas Iscariot who betrayed him

5 Jesus sent out these twelve
And giving them their instructions
He said
Do not take the road
To the Gentiles
Or enter a Samaritan town
6 But go rather to the lost sheep
Of the house of Israel

7
And preach on your way
Saying
The kingdom of the heavens
Has come close

8
Heal the sick
Raise the dead
Cleanse the lepers
Cast out demons

What you received as a free gift
Give as a free gift

9
Do not possess gold or silver
Or have small coins
In your belts
10
Or a bag for the road
Two tunics
Sandals
Or a staff
As the worker
Deserves his food

11
When you enter a town
Or a village
Make careful enquiries
As to who in it is deserving
And stay there until you leave

12
When you enter a house
Greet them

13 And if the house
Is indeed deserving
Let your peace come to it
But if it is not deserving
Let your peace
Return to you

14 And whoever does not receive you
Or hear your words
When you come outside that house
Or that town
Shake off the dust from your feet

15 Certainly I say to you
It will be more bearable
For the land of Sodom and Gomorrah
In the day of judgment
Than for that town

16 See how I
I send you out
As sheep among wolves
Therefore have the sense of serpents
And the simplicity of doves

The disciples will be persecuted

17 Guard against men
As they will hand you over
To councils
And they will scourge you
In their synagogues

18   You will be brought before
Governors and kings
For my sake
As a witness to them
And to the nations

19   But when they arrest you
Do not be anxious
About what you should say
Or how you should say it
Whatever you should say
Will be given to you

20   As it is not you who speak
But the spirit of your Father
Who is speaking in you

21   And a brother
Will betray a brother to death
And a father a child
And children
Will rise against parents
And will put them to death

22   Everyone will hate you
Because of my name
But whoever
Remains steadfast to the end
Will be saved

23   But when they persecute you
In one town

Escape to another
As certainly I say to you
By no means
Will you have passed through
All the towns of Israel
Before the Son of Man comes

24 A disciple
Is not above his teacher
Or a servant
Above his master

25 It is enough for the disciple
To be like his teacher
And the servant
Like his master

If they called the householder
Beelzebub
How much more
Those who belong to his house

The disciples should have courage

26 Therefore
You should not be afraid of them
As nothing has been covered
Which will not be revealed
Or is secret
Which will not be known

27 What I say to you
In darkness

81

You should tell in the light
And what you hear in your ear
Preach from the housetops

28   And do not be afraid
Of those who kill the body
But have no power
To kill the living soul

But rather be afraid
Of those who have the power
To destroy both soul and body
In the valley of burning

29   Are not two sparrows
Sold for a small copper coin
And not one of them
Will fall to earth
Without your Father

30   Even the hairs on your head
Are all counted

31   So do not be afraid
You are worth more
Than many sparrows

The disciples should follow Christ
32   Everyone who acknowledges me
In the presence of men

I myself
Will also acknowledge him
In the presence of my Father
In the heavens

33   And whoever disowns me
In the presence of men
I myself
Will also disown him
In the presence of my Father
In the heavens

34   Do not suppose
That I came to bring peace
On the earth
I did not come to bring peace
But a sword

35   As I came to cause disagreement
Between a man and his father
A daughter and her mother
A bride and her mother-in-law
36   And a man's enemies
Will be those in his house

37   The one
Who cares for father or mother
More than for me
Is not worthy of me
And the one
Who cares for son or daughter

More than for me
Is not worthy of me

38 The one
Who does not take his cross
And follow after me
Is not worthy of me

39 The one
Who finds his soul-bearing life
Will lose it
And the one
Who loses his soul-bearing life
For my sake
Will find it

40 The one
Who receives you
Receives me
And the one
Who receives me
Receives the one who sent me out

41 The one
Who receives a prophet
Because he is a prophet
Will obtain a prophet's reward
And the one
Who receives a just person
Because he is a just person
Will obtain a just person's reward

42   And whoever
        Gives one of these little ones
        Even a cup of cold water
        Because he is a disciple
        Certainly I say to you
        By no means
        Will he lose his reward

11 *Jesus answers John the Baptist*
1   And it happened
        That when Jesus had finished
        Giving his instructions
        To his twelve disciples
        He left there
        To teach and to preach
        In their towns

2   But when John heard in prison
        About the deeds of the Christ
        He sent his disciples to him
3   Who said
                Are you the one who is coming
                Or may we expect someone else?

4   Jesus answered them
                Go and give the news to John
                About what you hear and see

5   The blind have sight again
                And the lame walk
                Lepers are cleansed

The deaf hear
The dead are raised up
The poor receive the Gospel
6   And all who do not reject me
Are blessed

Jesus talks to the people about John
7   As they were leaving
Jesus began to talk to the crowds
About John
     And said
          What did you go out
          Into the desert
          To behold?
          A reed shaken by the wind?

8   But what did you go out
          To see?
          A man wearing fine clothes?
          Look how those who wear fine
              clothes
          Are in kings' houses

9   But why did you go out?
          Was it to see a prophet?
          I say to you
          Yes
          And more than a prophet

10   This is he
          Of whom it has been written

See how I myself
Send out my messenger
Before thy face
Who will make ready
Thy road in front of thee

11   Certainly I say to you
There has not risen up
Among those born of women
Anyone greater than John the Baptist
But the least
In the kingdom of the heavens
Is greater than he is

12   From the days of John the Baptist
Until now
The kingdom of the heavens
Gathers force
And the forceful take hold of it

13   Because all the prophets
And the Law
Prophesied until John

14   And if you are willing to receive him
He is Elijah
Who is about to come

15   Whoever has ears
Should hear

16   But to whom
      Shall I compare this generation?

      It is like children
      Sitting in the market
17   Who call to the others
      And say
      We piped to you
      And you did not dance

      We mourned
      And you did not beat your breasts

18   Because John
      Came neither eating nor drinking
      And they say
      He has a demon

19   The Son of Man
      Came eating and drinking
      And they say
      Look
      This is a man who is greedy
      And drinks wine
      A friend of tax-collectors
      And of outcasts

      But wisdom
      Is justified by her deeds

Jesus reproves the lakeside towns

20 Then he began to reproach the towns
   In which he had done
   Very many of his powerful deeds
   Because they did not change
   Their hearts and minds

21 Woe to you
   Chorazin
   Woe to you
   Bethsaida
   Because if the powerful deeds
   Had been done in Tyre and Sidon
   Which have been done in you
   They would have altered long ago
   Putting on sackcloth and ashes

22 However
   I say to you
   It will be more bearable
   For Tyre and Sidon
   At the day of judgment
   Than for you

23 And you
   Capernaum
   Were you lifted up
   As far as heaven?
   You shall go down
   As far as Hades
   Because if the powerful deeds

Had been done in Sodom
Which have been done in you
It would have remained
Until today

24 However
I say to you
It will be more bearable
For the land of Sodom
At the day of judgment
Than for you

Jesus prays to the Father
25 At that moment
Jesus responded by saying
I give praise to you
Father
Lord of heaven
And of earth
Because you have hidden these things
From the wise and the able
And have revealed them to babes
26 Yes
Father
As thus it was pleasing to you

The weary will find rest
27 Everything was handed over to me
By my Father
And no one really knows the Son
Except the Father

> Nor does anyone really know the
>   Father
> Except the Son
> And the one to whom
> It is the will of the Son
> To reveal him

28
> Come to me
> All who are growing weary
> And on whom
> Burdens have been laid
> And I myself
> Will rest you

29
> Take my yoke on you
> And learn from me
> Because I am gentle
> And humble in heart
> And you will find rest
> For the life of your souls

30
> As my yoke is easy
> And my burden is light

12 *In the cornfields on the sabbath*
1
At that season
Jesus was passing through the cornfields
On the sabbath

As his disciples were hungry
They began to pick ears of corn
And to eat them

2 But when the Pharisees saw this
    They said to him
        Look how your disciples
        Are doing something
        Which it is not lawful
        To do on the sabbath

3   And he said to them
        Have you not read
        What David did
        When he was hungry
        As were those with him?

4   How he entered the house of God
        And ate the loaves of offering
        Which it was not lawful
        For him to eat
        Nor for those with him
        But only for the priests?

5   Or have you not read
        In the Law
        That on the sabbath
        The priests in the Temple
        Profane the sabbath
        And are not to blame?

6   But I say to you
         That here
         There is something greater
         Than the Temple

7   If you had been aware
         What this is
         I wish mercy
         And not sacrifice
         You would not have condemned
         Those who are blameless
8   As the Son of Man
         Is also lord of the sabbath

Healing of a man with a withered hand

9   Then he left
         And went into their synagogue

10   And now there was a man
         Whose hand had wasted away

              So that they could accuse him
              They asked him
                   Is it lawful
                   To heal on the sabbath?

11   He said to them
              Is there a man among you
              Who has one sheep
              And if it falls into a pit
              On the sabbath

Will not take hold of it
And pull it out?

12   How much more is a man worth
Than a sheep?

Therefore it is lawful
To do what is right
On the sabbath

13   Then he said to the man
Stretch out your hand

He stretched it out
And it was made good
As healthy as was the other

14   When they went outside
The Pharisees
Considered how to proceed against him
So that they could destroy him

15   But Jesus was aware of this
And went away from there

Many people are healed
Many people followed him
And he healed them all
16   Telling them sternly
Not to make him known

94

17 So that what was said
Through the prophet Isaiah
Might be fulfilled

18 *See my servant*
Whom I have chosen
My beloved
In whom my living soul rejoiced

I will put my spirit upon him
And he will announce judgment
To the nations

19 *He will not quarrel*
Or cry out
Nor will anyone in the street
Hear his voice

20 *He will not break a reed*
Which has been bruised
Nor put out
The smoking wick
Until he brings judgment to victory

21 *And in his name*
Will the nations hope

Jesus heals a demoniac and reproves the Pharisees
22 A man was brought to him
Possessed by a demon
Who was both blind and dumb

And he healed him
So that the dumb man
Could both speak and see

23 All the people were astonished
    And said
        Is not he
        The Son of David?

24 But when the Pharisees heard it
    They said
        He does not cast out demons
        Except through Beelzebub
        The ruler of the demons

25 As he knew what they were thinking
    Jesus said to them
        Every kingdom
        Divided against itself
        Is made a desert
        And every city or house
        Divided against itself
        Will not stand

26   And if Satan
        Casts out Satan
        He is divided against himself
        So how will his kingdom stand?

27   And if I
        I cast out the demons

Through Beelzebub
By whom do your sons
Cast them out?
Therefore
They shall be your judges

28   But if by the Spirit of God
       I
       I cast out the demons
       Then the kingdom of God
       Has come upon you

29   Or how has any one the power
       To enter a strong man's house
       And seize his equipment
       Unless he first ties up
       The strong man?
       And then he will plunder his house

30   He that is not with me
       Is against me
       And he
       Who does not gather with me
       Scatters

31   Therefore I say to you
       All sin and blasphemy
       Will be forgiven to men
       But the blasphemy of the spirit
       Will not be forgiven

32

And whoever speaks a word
Against the Son of Man
It will be forgiven him
But whoever speaks
Against the Holy Spirit
It will not be forgiven him
Neither in this age
Nor in the one which is coming

33

Either make the tree sound
And its fruit sound
Or make the tree rotten
And its fruit rotten
Because the tree
Is recognized by its fruits

34

Offspring of vipers
How have you the ability
To say something good
When you are evil?
Because the mouth speaks
Out of the overflowing heart

35

The good man
Out of good treasure
Brings out good things
And the evil man
Out of evil treasure
Brings out evil things

36   But I say to you
      That every idle word
      Which men speak
      Must be accounted for
      In the day of judgment
37   As by your words
      You will be justified
      Or by your words
      You will be condemned

The scribes and Pharisees ask for a sign

38 Then some of the scribes and Pharisees
        Said to him
            Teacher
            It is our wish
            To see a sign from you

39   But he answered them
            An evil and adulterous generation
            Looks for a sign
            And no sign
            Shall be given to it
            Except the sign
            Of the prophet Jonah

40   Just as Jonah
            Was three days
            And three nights
            In the belly of the whale
            So the Son of Man
            Will be three days

And three nights
In the heart of the earth

41

The population of Nineveh
Will rise up at the judgment
And condemn this generation
Because they changed
Their hearts and minds
At the preaching of Jonah
And now
Something greater than Jonah
Is here

42

The queen of the South
Will be raised at the judgment
And condemn this generation
Because she came
From the bounds of the earth
To hear the wisdom of Solomon
And now
Something greater than Solomon
Is here

43

Now when the unclean spirit
Goes out of a man
He passes through waterless places
Looking for rest
But he does not find it

44

Then he says
I will go back into my house

Which is where I came from
And when he returns
He finds it unoccupied
Having been swept and put in order

45 Then he enters in there to stay
Taking with him
Seven other spirits
More evil than himself
And the last state of that man
Is worse than the first

It will also be so
With this evil generation

The family of Jesus
46 While he was still speaking
To the people
His mother and his brothers
Were standing outside
Trying to speak to him

48 When he had been told this
He answered
Who is my mother
And who are my brothers?

49 Then he stretched out his hand
Towards his disciples
And said
See here is my mother

And here are my brothers
50 As whoever does the will
Of my Father in the heavens
Is my brother
And my sister
And my mother

13 *Parable of the sower*
1 On that day
Jesus went out of the house
And sat beside the sea

2 Large crowds gathered round him
So that he embarked on to a boat
And sat there
While all the people
Stood on the shore

3 He told them many things
In parables
And said
See how the sower
Went out to sow

4 As he sowed
Some seeds fell by the wayside
And the birds
Came and ate them

5 But others fell on rocky places
Where they did not have much earth

And they sprouted at once
Because they had no depth of earth
6   When the sun rose
They were scorched
And as they had no root
They dried out

7   Others fell among thorn bushes
And the thorns came up
And choked them

8   Others fell on cultivated ground
And yielded fruit
Some increased a hundred
Some sixty
And some thirty times

9   Whoever has ears to hear
Should hear

Seeing and hearing
10   The disciples
Came and said to him
Why do you speak to them
In parables?

11   And he answered them
Because it has been given
To you
To become aware of the mysteries
Of the kingdom of the heavens

But it has not been given
To them

12 Whoever has
To him will be given
More than he needs
But whoever has not
From him will be taken
Even what he has

13 Therefore
I speak to them in parables
Because seeing
They do not see
And hearing
They do not hear
Neither do they understand

14 In them the prophecy of Isaiah
Is indeed fulfilled
Which says
Hearing
You will hear
But in no way understand
And seeing
You will see
But in no way perceive
15 *For the heart of this people*
Has become insensitive
And their ears
Are hard of hearing

And their eyes
They have closed
Lest they should perceive
With the eyes
And hear
With the ears
And understand
With the heart
And turn back
And I will heal them

16 But blessed are your eyes
Because they see
And your ears
Because they hear

17 Certainly I say to you
That many prophets
And upright men
Longed to perceive what you see
And did not perceive it
And to hear what your hear
But did not hear it

The meaning of the sower

18 Therefore listen
To the parable of the sower

19 When anyone hears
The word of the kingdom
And does not understand it

Then the evil one comes
And takes possession
Of what was sown in his heart
This is the seed
Sown by the wayside

20   The seed sown in the rocky places
Is the one who hears the word
And at once
Receives it with joy

21   But having no root in himself
It is short-lived
And when difficulties come about
Or there is persecution
Because of the word
He gives up at once

22   The seed sown among thorn bushes
Is the one who hears the word
And the problems of the present age
And the deceit of riches
Choke the word
And it becomes unfruitful

23   The seed sown on cultivated ground
Is the one who hears the word
And understands it
He indeed yields fruit
Some increased a hundred
Some sixty
And some thirty times

Parable of the field of the world

24 He set before them
Another parable
   And said
      The kingdom of the heavens
      Is like a man
      Who sowed the proper seed
      In his field

25   But while everybody was sleeping
      His enemy came
      Sowed darnel between the wheat
      And went away

26   When the green blade sprouted
      And produced fruit
      The darnel also appeared

27   The householder's servants
      Came to him and said
      Sir
      Did you not sow the proper seed
      In your field
      Then where has the darnel come
         from?

28   And he said to them
      A man who is my enemy
      Has done this

So the servants said to him
Do you wish us
To go and collect them?

29   But he said to them
No
As in collecting the darnel
You might root up the wheat
With it
30   Leave them both to grow together
Until the harvest

At the harvest season
I will say to the reapers
First collect the darnel
And bind it in bundles
To be burnt
But gather the wheat
Into my barn

Parable of the mustard seed
31   He set before them
Another parable
    And said
        The kingdom of the heavens
        Is like a mustard seed
        Which a man took
        And sowed in his field

32   It is the smallest
        Of all the seeds

> But when it has grown
> It is larger than other vegetables
> Becoming a tree
> So that the birds of heaven
> Come and nest in the branches

Parable of the yeast

33   He told them
> Another parable
> > The kingdom of the heavens
> > Is like yeast
> > Which a woman took
> > And hid in three large measures
> > Of fine flour
> > Until it was all leavened

34 Jesus said all this to the people
> In parables
> And he said nothing to them
> Except in a parable
35 Thus fulfilling
> What was spoken through the prophet
> When he said
> *I will open my mouth in parables*
> *I will speak of things kept secret*
> *From the foundation of the world*

36 Then he sent away the crowds
> And went into the house

The meaning of the field of the world
His disciples came to him
And said
Explain to us the parable
Of the darnel in the field

37   And he answered
The one sowing the proper seed
Is the Son of Man
38   The field is the world
And the proper seed
That is the sons of the kingdom
The darnel
That is the sons of the evil one

39   The enemy sowing it
Is the devil
The harvest
Is the end of the age
And the reapers
Are the angels

40   Therefore
As the darnel is collected
And burnt in the fire
That is how it will be
At the end of the age
41   When the Son of Man
Will send out his angels
And they will collect
From out of his kingdom

All offences
And all who break the law
42 And will throw them
Into the furnace of fire

There will be weeping
And gnashing of teeth

43 Then those who did what was right
Will shine out like the sun
In the kingdom of their Father

Whoever has ears
Should hear

Parable of the treasure
44 The kingdom of the heavens
Is like treasure hidden in a field
Which when a man found
He hid it
And in his joy
He went and sold everything he had
And bought that field

Parable of the pearl
45 Again
The kingdom of the heavens
Is like a merchant
Searching for fine pearls
46 When he found one pearl
Of great value

He went away
And sold everything he had
And bought it

Parable of the net

47 Again
The kingdom of the heavens
Is like a fishing net
Which was cast into the sea
Gathering all kinds
48 When it was filled
And brought up on to the beach
The fishermen sat down
And the wholesome fish
Were sorted into buckets
But the worthless were thrown away

49 That is how it will be
At the end of the age
The angels will go out
And will separate the evil doers
From among those who do right
50 And will throw them
Into the furnace of fire

There will be weeping
And gnashing of teeth

51 Have you understood
All these things?

They said to him
>> Yes

52 So he said to them
>> Therefore every scribe
>> Who is made a disciple
>> In the kingdom of the heavens
>> Is like a man
>> Who is a householder
>> And who brings out of his treasure
>> Both the new
>> And the old

Jesus is not accepted in his native place
53 And it happened
That when Jesus
Had reached the end
Of these parables
He went away from there

54 When he came to his native place
He taught them in their synagogues
So that they were astonished
>> And said
>>> From where has he the wisdom
>>> And the powerful deeds?

55 >> Is he not the carpenter's son
>> And is not his mother called Mary
>> And are not his brothers
>> James and Joseph

Simon and Judas
And are not his sisters
All here with us?

56   From where has he
All these things?

57 And they would not accept him

But Jesus said to them
A prophet
Is not without honour
Except in his native place
And in his own house

58 There
He did not perform
Many powerful deeds
Because of their lack of faith

14 *The death of John the Baptist*
1   It was at that season
When Herod the Tetrarch
Heard reports about Jesus
2   And said to his attendants
This is John the Baptist
He has risen from the dead
And therefore these powerful deeds
Are active in him

3 Herod had taken John
   And bound him captive in prison
   Because of Herodias
   The wife of his brother Philip

4 As John had said to him
   It is not lawful
   For you to have her

5 Although he wanted to kill him
   He was afraid of the people
   Because they held him
   To be a prophet

6 When Herod's birthday came
   Herodias' daughter
   Danced in front of them
   And pleased Herod

7 So that with an oath
   He promised to give her
   Whatever she would ask

8 So being led on
   By her mother
           Give me
       She said
           Here on a dish
           The head of John the Baptist

9 The King was distressed
   But because of his oath

And those at the table with him
He ordered that it should be given
10 And sent and beheaded John
In the prison

11 His head
Was brought on a dish
And given to the young girl
Who brought it to her mother

12 His disciples came up
And took the corpse
Which they buried

Then they came and brought the news
To Jesus

Feeding of the five thousand
13 When Jesus heard it
He went away on his own
By boat
And came to a desert place

Hearing of this
The people followed him on foot
From out of the towns
14 So that on landing
He saw a large crowd
And he had compassion on them
And healed their sick

15   As the evening drew on
     The disciples came to him
          And said
               This is a desert place
               And the hour is late
               Send the crowds away
               Into the villages
               To buy for themselves

16   But Jesus said to them
               It is not necessary
               For them to go away
               You give them something to eat

17   They answered him
               We have nothing here
               Except five loaves
               And two fish

18   And he said
               Bring them here to me

19   When he had ordered the crowds
     To sit down on the grass
     He took the five loaves
     And the two fishes
     And looking up to heaven
     He blessed
     And broke them

Then he gave the loaves
To the disciples
And the disciples
Gave them to the people

20 They all ate
And were satisfied
And they collected the fragments left over
Twelve wicker baskets full

21 Those who had eaten
Were about five thousand men
Apart from the women and children

Jesus is seen walking on the sea
22 Then he demanded that his disciples
Should embark on to the boat
And go ahead of him
To the other side
While he sent away the crowds

23 When he had sent the people away
He went up by himself
On the mountain
To pray
And when the evening came
He was there alone

24 But the boat
Was now far away from the land

118

Tossed by the waves
As the wind was contrary

25 In the fourth watch of the night
He came towards them
Walking on the sea

26 When the disciples saw him
Walking on the sea
They were troubled
    And said
        It is a phantom

And they cried out in fear

27 But Jesus spoke to them at once
    And said
        Be brave
        I
        I AM
        Do not be afraid

28   Peter said to him
        Lord
        If it is you
        Order me to come to you
        On the water

29   And he said
        Come

Lowering himself out of the boat
Peter walked on the water
And came close to Jesus

30   But when he saw
The strength of the wind
He was afraid
And beginning to sink
    He cried out
        Lord
        Save me

31   At once
Jesus stretched out his hand
And taking hold of him
    He said
        You have little faith
        Why did you doubt?

32   As they got into the boat
The wind dropped

33   Those who were in the boat
Bowed down before him
    Saying
        It is true
        You are God's son

Jesus heals many who are sick
34   They crossed over
And came to Gennesaret

35 When they recognized him
The inhabitants of the place
Sent out into the whole surroundings
And brought to him
All those who had fallen ill

36 And asked him to allow them
Only to touch the fringe of his cloak
And all who touched it
Recovered

15 *Clean and unclean*

1 Then Pharisees and scribes from Jerusalem
Came to Jesus
And said

2 Why do your disciples
Not keep the tradition of the elders
As they do not wash their hands
Whenever they eat bread?

3 And he answered them
Why do you yourselves
Not keep the commandment of God
Because of your tradition?

4 As God said
Honour your father and your mother
And whoever speaks evil
Of father or mother
Let him die the death

5 But you say
  Whoever says to his father or mother
  What might be due to you
  From me
  Is offered to the Temple
6 Certainly he does not honour
  His father or his mother

  You have set aside
  The word of God
  Because of your tradition

7 Hypocrites
  It was right what Isaiah
  Prophesied about you
  When he said
8 *This people*
  Honour me with their lips
  But their heart
  Is far from me away
9 *They worship me in vain*
  Teaching as doctrine
  The commandments of men

     forward
10 He called the crowd to him
  And said to them
   You should listen
   And understand

11   It is not what enters the mouth
       Which makes a man unclean   *degrades*
       But what comes out of the mouth

Then

12 The disciples came to him   *approaching*
       And said   *say to him*
         Do you know
         That the Pharisees
         Heard your words
         And were offended?

13   And he answered
         Every plantation
         Which my heavenly Father
         Has not planted
         Will be uprooted

14   Leave them   *Disregard*
         They are blind leaders of the blind
         And if a blind man
         Leads a blind man
         Both will fall into a pit

15   Peter said to him
         Make this parable
         Clear to us

16   So he said
         Are you also
         Without understanding?
         Do you not grasp

17   That everything entering the mouth
        Goes into the stomach
        And is cast out into the drain?

18   But what comes out of the mouth
        Comes from the heart
        And that
        Is what makes a man unclean   *degrades*

19   Out of the heart
        Come forth   *Enmity against the lives of*
        Evil thoughts   *impurity in human oth*
        And murders and adulteries *relationships*
Uncleanliness of Fornications and thefts
soul   False witness and blasphemies

20   These are the things
        Which make a man unclean   *degrade*
        But eating with unwashed hands
        Does not make a man unclean

        Healing of the daughter of the Canaanite woman
21   Jesus left there
        And went to the region
        Of Tyre and Sidon

22   And now
        There came a Canaanite woman
        From that district
            Who cried out
                Pity me

Lord
Son of David
My daughter is possessed of a demon
And has it badly

23 But he did not answer a word

And his disciples came
And begged him
Saying
Send her away
Because she is calling out behind us

24 He replied to them
I have only been sent
To the lost sheep
Of the house of Israel

25 She came however
And bowing down
She said
Lord
Help me

26 He answered
It is not right
To take the children's bread
And throw it to the household dogs

27 And she said
Yes

Lord
But even the household dogs
Eat the crumbs
Which fall from their master's table

28   Then Jesus replied to her
          O woman
          You have great faith
          It shall be as you wish

And at that hour
Her daughter was healed

Feeding of the four thousand
29   Jesus went away from there
And passing the sea of Galilee
He went up into a mountain
Where he sat down

30   And large crowds came to him
Bringing with them
The lame
The maimed
The blind
The dumb
And many others

They laid them at his feet
And he healed them

31   So that the people were astonished
When they saw
The dumb speaking
The maimed whole
The lame walking
The blind seeing
And they praised the God of Israel

32   Then Jesus
Called his disciples to him
     And said
          I have compassion on the crowd
          Because they have been with me
          Three days
          And have nothing to eat
          I am unwilling
          To send them away hungry
          As they might faint on the road

33   His disciples said to him
          We are here in a wilderness
          From where
          Could we get enough bread
          To satisfy so many people?

34   Jesus said to them
          How many loaves
          Have you?

And they said
    Seven
    And a few little fishes

35 Then he ordered the crowd
To sit down on the ground

36 Taking the seven loaves
And the fish
He gave thanks
And broke them

Then he gave them to the disciples
And the disciples
Gave them to the people

37 They all ate
And were satisfied
Then they filled seven reed baskets
With the fragments left over
Which they took up

38 Those who had eaten
Were about four thousand men
Besides women and children

39 When he had sent away the crowds
He embarked on to a boat
And came to the district of Magadan

16 *The Pharisees and Sadducees ask for a sign*

1   The Pharisees and Sadducees
     Came to him to tempt him
     And asked him to show them
     A sign from heaven

2   But he answered them
             When evening comes
             You say
             It will be fair weather
             As the sky is red
3   But in the morning
             It will be stormy today
             As the sky is red and overcast

         You are able to interpret
         The face of heaven
         But not the signs
         Of the moment in time

4   An evil and adulterous generation
         Looks for a sign
         But no sign
         Shall be given to it
         Except the sign of Jonah

     Then he left them
     And went away

Jesus warns against the teaching of the Pharisees

5   When the disciples
Came to the other side
They had forgotten to take any bread

And Jesus said to them
6   Watch out
And guard against the yeast
Of the Pharisees and Sadducees

7   But they discussed it
Among themselves
Saying
We did not bring any bread

8   As he was aware of this
Jesus said
You that have little faith
Why do you discuss among
yourselves
That it is
Because you have no bread?

9   Do you not understand
Neither remember
The five loaves
Of the five thousand
And how many wicker baskets
You took up?

10   Nor the seven loaves
        Of the four thousand
        And how many reed baskets
        You took up?

11   Why do you not understand
        That I was not speaking to you
        About bread
        But to guard against the yeast
        Of the Pharisees and Sadducees

12 Then they understood
    That he did not say
    They should guard against the yeast
    But against the teaching
    Of the Pharisees and Sadducees

Christ's charge to Peter

13 When Jesus
    Came into the region of Caesarea Philippi
        He asked his disciples
            Whom do men believe
            The Son of Man
            To be?

14   And they said
        Some indeed
        John the Baptist
        Others Elijah
        And others Jeremiah
        Or one of the prophets

15   He said to them
       But you
       Whom do you believe
       Me to be?

16   Simon Peter answered
       You are the Christ
       The Son of the living God

17   Jesus answered him
       You are blessed
       Simon Bar-Jona
       Because flesh and blood
       Have not revealed it to you
       But my Father in the heavens

18   And I tell you myself
       That you are Peter
       And on this rock
       I will build my community
       And the gates of the underworld
       Will not hold out against it

19   I will give you the keys
       Of the kingdom of the heavens
       And whatever you bind on earth
       It shall be
       As having been bound in the heavens
       And whatever you release on earth
       It shall be
       As having been released in the heavens

20 Then he warned his disciples
    That they should not tell anyone
    That he is the Christ

First prophecy of the Passion
21 From then on
    Jesus Christ
    Began to show to his disciples
    That it would be necessary for him
    To go to Jerusalem
    And to endure much suffering
    From the elders
    And chief priests and scribes
    To be killed
    And to be raised
    On the third day

22 Taking him aside
    Peter began to speak sternly to him
        And said
            May mercy be on you
            Lord
            This must not happen to you

23 But he turned
        And said to Peter
            Go behind me
            Satan
            You would cause my downfall
            Because you are not thinking

Of the concerns of God
But of the concerns of men

24   Then Jesus
Said to his disciples
        If any one
        Is willing to come after me
        He should not consider himself
        But take his cross
        And follow me

25   For whoever wishes to save
        His soul-bearing life
        Will lose it
        And whoever loses
        His soul-bearing life
        For my sake
        Will find it

26   What use is it to a man
        To gain the whole world
        And suffer the loss
        Of his living soul?

        Or what will a man give
        As the price
        Of his living soul?

27   When the Son of Man comes
        Revealing the glory of his Father
        And his angels

>Then he will reward each one
>According to what he has done

28 Certainly I say to you
>That there are some standing here
>Who will surely not taste death
>Until they see the Son of Man
>Coming in his kingdom

17 *The Transfiguration*

1 After six days
>Jesus
>Took Peter
>With James and his brother John
>And brought them by themselves
>Up on to a high mountain

2 He was transformed
>In their presence
>His face shone like the sun
>And his clothing
>Became white as the light

3 And now
>Moses and Elijah
>Were seen by them
>Talking with him

4 Peter said to Jesus
>Lord
>It is right

For us to be here
If you wish
I will put up three tents here
One for you
One for Moses
And one for Elijah

5   While he was speaking
A bright cloud overshadowed them
    And a voice out of the cloud said
      This is my son
      The beloved
      In whom I rejoiced
      Listen to him

6   On hearing this
The disciples fell on their faces
And were very much afraid

7   Jesus came and touched them
    And said
      Get up
      And do not be afraid

8   As they lifted up their eyes
They saw no one
Except Jesus himself

9   And coming down from the mountain
    Jesus instructed them
      Do not tell anyone

About the vision
Until the Son of Man
Has been raised from the dead

10 Then the disciples asked him
Why do the scribes
Say that Elijah must come first?

11 And he answered
Indeed Elijah does come
And will restore everything
12 But I say to you
That Elijah has come already
And they failed to recognize him
But did to him
Whatever they wanted
So also the Son of Man
Is about to suffer from them

13 Then the disciples understood
That he spoke to them
About John the Baptist

Healing of the demoniac boy
14 When they reached the crowd
A man came to him
And kneeling in front of him
15 He said
Lord
Have pity on my son
Because he is lunatic

137

And has it badly
As often he falls into the fire
And often into the water

16   I brought him to your disciples
And they were not able
To heal him

17   Jesus answered
O faithless and perverse generation
How long
Shall I be with you?
How long
Shall I endure you?
Bring him here to me

18   When Jesus spoke to it sternly
The demon came out of him
And from that hour
The boy was healed

19   The disciples
Came to Jesus on their own
And said
Why were we not able
To cast it out?

20   And he said to them
Because of your little faith
Certainly I say to you
If your faith is as much

As a mustard seed
You will say to this mountain
Move over to there
And it will be removed
And nothing
Will be impossible for you

Second prophecy of the Passion
22 As they remained in Galilee
Jesus said to them
The Son of Man
Is about to be betrayed
Into the hands of men
23 They will kill him
And on the third day
He will be raised

They were very much distressed

The tax money
24 When they came to Capernaum
Those who collected
The half drachma Temple tax
Went up to Peter
And said
Does not your teacher
Pay the tax?

He said
Yes he does

25 He came into the house
And Jesus spoke to him at once
And said
How does it seem to you
Simon?
From whom
Do the kings of the earth
Take toll or tax?
From their sons
Or from strangers?

26 So he said
From strangers

And Jesus said to him
Then the sons are free

27 But so as not to offend them
Go to the sea
Cast a hook
And take the first fish
That comes up
On opening its mouth
You will find a silver shekel
Take that
And give it to them
For me and for you

18 *The disciples' question*

1   In that hour
The disciples came to Jesus
    And said
      Then who is the greatest
      In the kingdom of the heavens?

2   And calling a little child
To come to them
He placed it in their midst
3   And said
      Certainly I say to you
      Unless you turn
      And become like the children
      By no means will you enter
      The kingdom of the heavens

4   Therefore
    Whoever humbles himself
    Like this child
    Is the greatest
    In the kingdom of the heavens

5   And whoever receives
    One such child
    In my name
    Receives me

6   But whoever causes the downfall
    Of one of these little ones
    Who believe in me

It would be to his advantage
If a great mill-stone
Were hung round his neck
And he was drowned
In an ocean of sea

7   Woe to the world
On account of its pitfalls
It is necessary that temptations come
But woe to that man
Through whom the temptation comes

8   If your hand or your foot
Causes your downfall
Cut it off
And throw it away from you
It is right for you
To enter into Life
Maimed or lame
Rather than having two hands
Or two feet
To be thrown into the fire
That burns throughout the ages

9   If your eye
Causes your downfall
Pluck it out
And throw it away from you
It is right for you
To enter one-eyed into Life
Rather than having two eyes

To be thrown
Into the retribution of fire

10   Make sure
That you do not despise
One of these little ones
For I say to you
That in the heavens
Their angels
Always see the face of my Father
In the heavens

11   For the Son of Man
Came to save the lost

Parable of the lost sheep

12   How does it seem to you?
If any man
Has a hundred sheep
And one of them strays away
Will he not leave
The ninety-nine in the mountains
And go to look for the wanderer?

13   And if it happens
That he finds it
Certainly I say to you
That he rejoices more
Over that one
Than over the ninety-nine
That did not stray

14   So before the face of your Father
      In the heavens
      It is not the intention
      That one of these little ones
      Should be lost

Teaching for the disciples

15   If your brother does wrong
      Go and tell him
      When you are alone with him
      If he listens to you
      You have gained your brother

16   But if he does not listen
      Take one or two people with you
      That on the evidence
      Of two or three witnesses
      All that is said
      May be confirmed

17   And if he refuses
      To listen to them
      Tell the assembly
      Then let him be to you
      As a Gentile and a tax-collector

18   Certainly I say to you
      Whatever you bind on earth
      Shall be
      As having been bound in heaven
      And what ever you release on earth

Shall be
As having been released in heaven

19 Again I say to you
That if two of you agree
On the earth
About any concern
For which you ask
So it shall be for you
From my Father in the heavens

20 For when two or three
Have come together
In my name
There
I am in the midst of them

Parable of the unforgiving servant

21 Then Peter
Came to him and said
Lord
If my brother wrongs me
How often should I forgive him?
As often as seven times?

22 Jesus said to him
I do not tell you
As often as seven times
But as often as seventy times seven

23 Therefore the kingdom of the heavens
Is like a man
Who was a king
And who wished to settle accounts
With his servants

24 And as he began the reckoning
Someone was brought to him
Who owed him
Ten thousand talents weight
Of silver pieces

25 As he could not pay
The lord gave orders
That he should be sold
Together with his wife
And his children
And everything that he had
So that the debt should be repaid

26 Then the servant
Fell down and implored him
Saying
Wait with your fury against me
And I will repay you everything

27 Filled with compassion
The lord of that servant
Released him
And forgave him the debt

28   But when he went out
That servant
Found one of his fellow servants
Who owed him a hundred denarii
And choking him
He said
Repay what you owe

29   Then his fellow servant
Fell down and begged him
Saying
Wait with your fury against me
And I will repay you

30   He would not wait
But went away
And threw him into prison
Until he should repay what was owing

31   When his fellow servants
Saw what took place
They were much distressed
And went to their lord
To make clear to him
Everything that had happened

32   Summoning him
His lord said
You wicked servant
I forgave you your debt
Because you begged me

33   Should you not have had pity
        On your fellow servant
        As I myself pitied you?

34   His lord was angry
        And handed him over
        To the tormentors
        Until he should repay
        Everything that he owed

35   This my heavenly Father
        Will also do to you
        Unless each one of you
        Forgives his brother
        From his heart

19   *A discussion about marriage*
1   Now it happened
        That when Jesus
        Had finished speaking these words
        He left Galilee
        And came into the district of Judea
        Across the Jordan
2   Large crowds followed him
        And he healed them there

3   Pharisees came to him
        To test him
                And said
                        Are there any grounds

148

On which it is lawful
For a man to release his wife?

4   He answered
Have you not read
That from the beginning
The Creator
Made them male and female?

5   And he said
Because of this
A man should leave
His father and his mother
And be joined to his wife
The two
Shall be one flesh
6   So that they are no longer two
But one flesh

Therefore
What God joined together
Man should not separate

7   They said to him
Then why did Moses
Command us
To provide a document of divorce
For her release

8   He said to them
It was because

Of your unyielding hearts
That Moses
Allowed you to release your wives
But from the beginning
It was not so

9   Now I say to you
That whoever releases his wife
Except for immorality
And marries another
Commits adultery

10   The disciples said to him
If this is the relationship
Between a man and his wife
It is not an advantage
To marry

11   And he said to them
Not everyone
Can accept these words
But only those
To whom it has been given

12   Some
Were born from a mother's womb
Incapable of marriage
And some
Were made incapable by men
And some
Made themselves incapable

For the sake
Of the kingdom of the heavens

Whoever can accept this
Let him accept it

Children are brought to Jesus
13 Then children were brought to him
So that he
Might put his hands on them
And pray
But the disciples reproved them

14 So Jesus said
Allow the children
To come to me
And do not hinder them
For of such as they are
Is the kingdom of the heavens

15 He put his hands on them
And went away from there

The rich young man
16 Then
Someone came up to him
And said
Teacher
What good that I do
Would enable me to have life
Throughout the ages?

Jesus said to him
17   Why do you ask me
    What is good?
    There is one who is good
    But if you wish
    To enter into life
    Keep the commandments

18   He said to him
    Which?

And Jesus said
    You shall not kill
    You shall not commit adultery
    You shall not steal
    You shall not witness falsely
    Honour your father and your mother
19   And you shall love your neighbour
    As yourself

20   The young man said to him
    I have kept all these things
    How do I fall short?

21   Jesus said to him
    If you wish to be perfect
    Go and sell what belongs to you
    To give to the poor
    You will have treasure in heaven
    Then come and follow me

22 When the young man
    Heard these words
    He went sadly away
    As he had extensive possessions

23   So Jesus said to his disciples
            Certainly I say to you
            That a rich man
            Will have difficulty
            In entering the kingdom of the
                heavens

24   And again I say to you
            It is easier for a camel
            To pass
            Through the eye of a needle
            Than for a rich man
            To enter the kingdom of God

25 When the disciples heard this
    They were absolutely astonished
            And said
                Who then
                Is able to be saved?

26   Gazing into them
            Jesus said
                With men
                This is impossible
                But with God
                Everything is possible

27   Peter said to him
          Look how we have left everything
          And followed you
          Then what shall we have?

28   And Jesus said to them
          Certainly I say to you
          That at the rebirth
          When the Son of Man
          Sits on his throne of glory
          You who have followed me
          Will yourselves
          Also sit on twelve thrones
          Judging the twelve tribes of Israel

29   And everyone
          Who has left houses
          Or brothers or sisters
          Or father or mother
          Or children or lands
          For the sake of my name
          Will receive many times more
          And will inherit life
          Throughout the ages
30   But many first
          Will be last
          And the last first

20 *Parable of the workers in the vineyard*
1   As the kingdom of the heavens
          Is like a man

154

Who was a householder
And went out
Early in the morning
To hire workers for his vineyard

2   He agreed with the workers
For a denarius a day
And sent them into his vineyard

3   At about the third hour
He went out
And saw others
Standing in the market
Doing nothing

4   He said to them
You also
Should go into the vineyard
And I will pay you
Whatever is just

So they went

5   Again
He went out
At about the sixth
And the ninth hour
And did the same

6   Going out
At about the eleventh hour

He found others standing there
And said to them
Why do you stand here all day
Doing nothing?

7
They said
Because no-one has hired us

He said to them
You also
Should go into the vineyard

8
When it was evening
The lord of the vineyard
Said to his bailiff
Call the workers
And pay their wages
Beginning with the last
Up to the first

9
When those came
Who had been hired
At about the eleventh hour
They each received a denarius

10
When the first came
They thought
That they would receive more
But they also
Each received a denarius

11   On receiving it
       They grumbled about the householder
       And said
12   Those who came last
       Worked for one hour
       And you
       Have made them equal to us
       Who have borne the burden
       And the searing heat
       Of the day

13   But he answered one of them
       Companion
       I am not unjust to you
       Did you not agree with me
       For a denarius?

14   Take what is yours
       And go
       I wish to give to this last one
       The same
       As I have given to you

15   Is it not lawful
       For me to do what I wish
       With what is mine?
       Or is your cye evil
       Because I
       I am good?

16   Thus the last will be first
      And the first last

Third prophecy of the Passion
17   When Jesus
      Was about to go up to Jerusalem
      He took the twelve disciples
      On their own
          And on the road
          He said to them
18   See how we are going up
              To Jerusalem
              And the Son of Man
              Will be handed over
              To the chief priests and scribes
              And they
              Will condemn him to death

19   They will deliver him
              To the Gentiles
              To be mocked
              And scourged
              And crucified
              And on the third day
              He will be raised

The mother of James and John asks a favour
20   Then the mother of Zebedee's sons
      Came to him
      With her sons

She bowed down
And asked him for something

21   He said to her
        What do you want?

    She said to him
        Say that these my two sons
        May sit
        One on your right
        And one on your left
        In your kingdom

22   Jesus answered
        You do not know
        What you ask
        Are you able to drink the cup
        Which I myself
        Am about to drink?

    They said to him
        We are able

23   He said to them
        Indeed you shall drink my cup
        But to sit on my right
        And on my left
        This is not mine to give
        But is for those
        For whom it has been prepared
        By my Father

24 When the ten heard this
They were indignant
About the two brothers

25 So Jesus called them to him
And said
You know
That those who rule the Gentiles
Dominate them
And their great ones
Have authority over them

26 It is not so among you
But whoever among you
Wishes to become great
Will be the one who serves you

27 And whoever wishes
To be first among you
Will be your servant

28 As the Son of Man
Did not come to be served
But to serve
And to give his soul-bearing life
As ransom for many

Two blind men healed
29 As they left Jericho
A large crowd followed him

30 And now there were two blind men
Sitting beside the road
When they heard
That Jesus
Is passing by
They cried out
Lord
Pity us
Son of David

31 The crowd
Ordered them to be quiet
But they cried out
All the more
Lord
Pity us
Son of David

32 Jesus stood still
And calling them
He said
What do you want me
To do for you?

33 They said to him
Lord
That our eyes
May be opened

34 And filled with compassion
Jesus touched their eyes

And immediately
They could see again
And followed him

21   *The entry into Jerusalem*
1   When they drew near Jerusalem
And came to Bethphage
On the Mount of Olives
Then Jesus sent out two disciples
2   Saying to them
              Go into the village
              That is in front of you
              And immediately
              You will find an ass
              Tied up
              And a colt with her
              Untie them
              And bring them to me

3   And if anyone
              Says anything to you
              Say
              The Lord needs them
              And he will send them at once

4   This happened
So that what was spoken
Through the prophet
Might be fulfilled
When he said
5   *Tell the daughter of Zion*

162

See how your King comes to you
Gentle
And mounted on an ass
On a colt
Foal of a beast of burden

6 The disciples went
And did as Jesus
Had directed them

7 They brought the ass
And the colt
Putting on them their cloaks
On which he sat

8 The large crowd
Spread out their cloaks
On the road
And others cut branches from the trees
And spread them on the road

9 The crowds who went in front
And those who followed
Cried out
Hosanna
To the Son of David
Blest be the one who comes
In the name of the Lord
Hosanna
In the highest places

10 As he entered Jerusalem
The whole city was in uproar
    Saying
        Who is this?

11   And the crowds said
        This is the prophet Jesus
        From Nazareth in Galilee

Jesus clears the Temple
12 Jesus entered the Temple
And cast out
All who were selling
And were buying
In the Temple
He overturned
The tables of the money-changers
And the seats of those selling doves

13   And he said to them
        My house
        Shall be called
        A house of prayer
        But you
        Are making it
        A robber's cave

14 The blind and the lame
Came to him in the Temple
And he healed them

15 The chief priests and the scribes
Saw the wonders which he did
And the children in the Temple
    Who were calling out
        Hosanna to the Son of David

    And they were indignant
16 And said to him
    Do you hear
    What they are saying?

    Jesus said to them
    Yes
    Have you never read
    Out of the mouths
    Of little children
    And babes in arms
    Thou hast perfected praise

The fig tree
17 He left there
And went out of the city
To Bethany
And stayed overnight

18 Going up early to the city
He was hungry
19 And when he saw one fig tree
By the road
He went up to it
But found nothing except leaves

165

And he said to it
> May you never bear fruit
> Throughout the ages

And the fig tree
Was withered up instantly

20   When they saw it
The disciples were astonished
> And said
> > How was the fig tree
> > Withered up in an instant?

21   Jesus answered them
> Certainly I say to you
> If you believe
> And do not waver
> You will not only perform
> The sign of the fig tree
> But if you say to this mountain
> Be taken up
> And thrown into the sea
> It will be so

22   And all that you ask
> In prayer
> If you have faith
> You will receive it

Jesus questions the chief priests about John

23 He entered the Temple
And the chief priests
And the elders of the people
Came to him
While he was teaching
    And said
        By what authority
        Are you doing these things?
        And who gave you this authority?

24 Jesus answered them
        I will also ask you one question
        And if you answer me
        I will also tell you
        By what authority
        I do these things

25   Where did John's baptism come from?
        From heaven
        Or from men?

They discussed it among themselves
    If we say
    From heaven
    He will say to us
    Why then did you not believe him?

26   But if we say
    From men
    We are afraid of the people

As everyone believes John
To be a prophet

So they answered Jesus
We do not know

27 Then he said to them
Neither will I
I say to you
By what authority
I do these things

Parable of the two sons
28 What is your opinion?

A man had two children
He went to the first
And said
Child
Go and work in the vineyard today
29 He answered
I am going sir
But he did not go

30 Then he went to the second
And said the same
He answered
I will not
But later he changed his mind
And went

31   Which of the two
        Carried out
        The will of the father?

    They said
        The second

    Jesus said to them
        Certainly I say to you
        Tax-collectors and prostitutes
        Will go in front of you
        Into the kingdom of God

32   John came to you
        On a righteous path
        And you did not believe him
        But the tax-collectors
        And the prostitutes
        Believed him
        But you
        Seeing this
        Did not change your minds later
        And believe him

Parable of the wicked farmers
33   Hear another parable

        A man who owned property
        Planted a vineyard
        Set a hedge round it
        Dug in it a wine press

And built a watch tower
Then let it to farmers
And went out of the country

34 When it was almost the season
For the vintage
He sent his servants to the farmers
To receive the fruit

35 The farmers took his servants
And beat this one
Killed that one
And stoned another

36 Again
He sent out more servants
Than at first
And they treated them
In the same way

37 Later
He sent his son to them
As he said
They will respect my son

38 But when those farmers
Saw the son
They said to one another
This is the heir
Let us kill him
And take possession of the inheritance

39   They took him
And throwing him out
Outside of the vineyard
They killed him

40   Therefore
When the lord of the vineyard comes
What will he do to those farmers?

41   They said to him
He will utterly destroy those wicked
ones
And will let out the vineyard
To other farmers
Who will give up to him
The fruit in its season

42   Jesus said to them
Have you never read in the Scriptures
A stone which the builders rejected
Became the head of the corner
This comes from the Lord
And is wonderful in our eyes

43   I tell you
That because of this
The kingdom of God
Will be taken from you
And will be given to that nation
Which produces its fruits

44   Whoever
Falls on to this stone
Will be broken in pieces
But whoever
It falls on
Will be crushed to powder

45   When the chief priests and the Pharisees
Heard the parable
They were aware
That he was speaking about them

46   Then they tried to seize him
But were afraid of the crowds
Because they took him for a prophet

22 *Parable of the marriage of the king's son*
1   Jesus spoke to them again in parables
And said
2   The kingdom of the heavens
Is like a man who was king
And who made a marriage
For his son

3   He sent out his servants
To call those invited to the marriage
But they did not wish to come

4   Again
He sent out other servants
Saying

Tell those who were invited
Look
Now I have prepared my banquet
My oxen
And the fatted cattle
Have been slaughtered
Everything is ready
Come to the marriage

5   But they were unconcerned
And went away
One to his own fields
Another to his warehouse
6   And the rest
Took his servants
Insulted them
And killed them

7   The king became angry
And sent out his soldiers
To destroy those murderers
And set their city on fire

8   Then he said to his servants
Indeed the marriage is ready
But those who were invited
Were not worthy

9   Therefore go out to the crossroads
And call to the marriage
All whom you find

10   And those servants
        Went out on to the roads
        And gathered all whom they found
        Both the wicked and the good
        And in the wedding hall
        The tables were filled

11   But when the king entered
        To behold those who were feasting
        He saw there a man
        Who had not been dressed
        In a wedding garment

12   And he said to him
        Companion
        How did you come in here
        Without having a wedding garment?

        And he was silenced

13   Then the king
        Said to those who were serving
        Tie his feet
        And his hands
        And throw him out
        Into the outer darkness

        There will be weeping
        And gnashing of teeth

14   For many are called
      But few are chosen

      The Pharisees' question
15   Then the Pharisees
      Went and considered
      How they could trap him
      In what he said

16   So they sent their disciples
      With the Herodians to him
          And they asked
              Teacher
              We know that you are truthful
              And in truth
              Teach the way of God
              And that no-one's position
              Matters to you
              As you do not look
              At the status of men

17   Therefore tell us
              How it seems to you
              Is it lawful or not
              To pay the tax to Caesar?

18   But Jesus
      Was aware of their wickedness
          And said
              Why do you hypocrites

Tempt me?
19 Show me the tax money

And they brought him
A denarius

20 So he said to them
Of whom is this portrait?
And of whom the inscription?

21 They said
It is Caesar's

Then he said to them
Therefore
Give back to Caesar
What belongs to Caesar
And to God
What belongs to God

22 They were astonished
At what they heard
And leaving him
They went away

The Sadducees' question
23 On that same day
Sadducees
Who say that there is no resurrection
Came to him
And asked the question

24   Teacher
        Moses said
        If any man dies
        Who has no children
        Then afterwards
        His brother shall marry the wife
        And raise up descendants
        To his brother

25   Now seven brothers
        Were with us
        The first
        Married and died
        As he had no children
        He left his wife to his brother
26   It was the same with the second
        And the third
        Until the seventh

27   Last of all
        The woman died

28   In the resurrection
        Whose wife of the seven
        Will she be?
        Because all of them had her

29   Jesus answered them
            You are wrong
            You neither know the Scriptures
            Nor the power of God

30   Because in the resurrection
        They neither marry
        Nor are given in marriage
        But are like the angels
        In heaven

31   Concerning the resurrection of the
            dead
        Have you not read
        What was told to you by God
32   When he said
        I
        I AM the God of Abraham
        And the God of Isaac
        And the God of Jacob

        He is not the God
        Of the dead
        But of the living

33   The crowds who heard him
     Were astonished at his teaching

     The lawyer's question
34   When the Pharisees
     Heard that he had silenced
     The Sadducees
     They met together
35   And one of them
     Who was a lawyer
         Put this question to him

To tempt him
36   Teacher
Which is the great commandment
In the Law?

37   And he said to him
You shall love the Lord your God
With all your heart
And with all your soul
And with all your mind

38   This is the great
And first
Commandment

39   The second is like it
You shall love your neighbour
As yourself

40   On these two commandments
Hang all the Law
And the prophets

Jesus questions the Pharisees
41 When the Pharisees
Had gathered together
    Jesus
Asked them a question
42   What is your opinion of Christ
Of whom is he the son?

They said to him
Of David

43 He said to them
Then how is David in spirit
Able to call him Lord
Saying
44 *The Lord*
Said to my Lord
Sit on my right
Until I put your enemies
Under your feet

45 Then if David
Calls him Lord
How is he his son?

46 And no-one was able
To answer a word to him
Nor from that day
Did anyone
Dare to question him any more

23 *Condemnation of the scribes and the Pharisees*
1 Then Jesus
Spoke to the crowds and his disciples
2 And said
The scribes and the Pharisees
Sit on Moses' seat
3 Therefore you must obey them
And do whatever they tell you

But do not perform their deeds
For what they say
Is not what they do

4   They bind heavy burdens
Which are hard to bear
And lay them on men's shoulders
But they are not willing
To move them with their finger

5   They do all their deeds
So that men may behold them
They broaden the little leather prayer
   boxes
Worn on the forehead and the arm
And lengthen the tassels
On their cloaks

6   They like the best places
At meals
And the first seats
In the synagogues
7   And greetings in the public places
And to be called Rabbi
By men

8   But you
Should not be called Rabbi
As you have one teacher
And you are all brothers
9   And call no-one your father

On the earth
As there is one
Who is your heavenly Father
10   Neither should you
Be called leader
Because you have one leader
The Christ

11   The greatest among you
Should serve you
12   And whoever exalts himself
Will be humbled
Whoever humbles himself
Will be exalted

13   Woe to you
Scribes and Pharisees
Hypocrites
Because you close
The kingdom of the heavens
Against men
And you do not go in yourselves
Nor allow those who would enter
To go in

14   Woe to you
Scribes and Pharisees
Hypocrites
Who eat up the inheritance of widows
And make pretence of long prayers
You will receive greater condemnation

15   Woe to you
Scribes and Pharisees
Hypocrites
Because you travel over the sea
And over dry land
To make one convert
And when he has been converted
You make him twice as much
A son of retribution
As yourselves

16   Woe to you
Blind guides
As you say
Whoever swears
By the shrine
That is nothing
But whoever swears
By the gold of the shrine
He is bound by his oath

17   Blind fools that you are
As which is greater
The gold
Or the shrine
Which consecrates the gold?

18   And whoever swears
By the altar of sacrifice
That is nothing
But whoever swears

By the gift upon it
Is bound by his oath
19 Blind that you are
For which is greater
The gift
Or the altar
Which consecrates the gift?

20 Therefore
Whoever swears
By the altar
Swears by it
And by all that is on it

21 And whoever swears
By the shrine
Swears by it
And by the one
Who dwells in it

22 And whoever swears
By heaven
Swears by the throne of God
And by the one
Who sits upon it

23 Woe to you
Scribes and Pharisees
Hypocrites
For you take a tenth of peppermint
Dill and cumin

And neglect
The weightier aspects of the Law
Judgment
Mercy and faith
You should do these things
While not neglecting the others

24 You blind guides
Who strain out the tiny insect
But swallow the camel

25 Woe to you
Scribes and Pharisees
Hypocrites
Because you clean the outside
Of the cup and the elegant dish
But inside
They are full of grasping
And excess

26 You blind Pharisees
First clean the inside
Of the cup
Then the outside
May also be clean

27 Woe to you
Scribes and Pharisees
Hypocrites
Because you are like graves
Which have been whitened

They indeed appear beautiful
On the outside
But inside
They are full
Of the bones of the dead
And all uncleanness

28 Thus outwardly
You appear to men to do what is right
But inwardly
You are full of hypocrisy
And law-breaking

29 Woe to you
Scribes and Pharisees
Hypocrites
Because you build the graves
Of the prophets
And adorn the tombs
Of the just
30 And say
If we had been present
In the days of our fathers
We would not have shared with them
In the blood of the prophets
31 You yourselves bear witness
That you are the sons
Of those who murdered the prophets
32 And you complete
The measure of your fathers

33   Serpents
        Offspring of vipers
        How will you flee
        From the judgment of retribution

34   Therefore
        See how I
        I send out to you
        Prophets
        And learned men
        And scribes

        Some of them
        You will kill and crucify
        Some of them
        You will scourge in your synagogues
        And will pursue
        From city to city

35   So that there will come upon you
        All the righteous blood
        Shed on the earth
        From the blood of righteous Abel
        To the blood of Zachariah
        Son of Barachiah
        Whom you murdered
        Between the shrine
        And the altar of sacrifice

36   Certainly I say to you
      All these things
      Will come upon this generation

37   Jerusalem
      Jerusalem
      Who killed the prophets
      And stoned those sent out to her
      How often
      I wished to gather your children
      As a bird gathers her nestlings
      Under her wings
      But you would not

38   Look how your house
      Is left to you

39   Because I say to you
      It is certain that from now on
      You will not see me
      Until you say
      Blest be the one who comes
      In the name of the Lord

24 *Prophecies of war and persecution*
1   As Jesus went out of the Temple
      His disciples
      Came to show to him
      The buildings of the Temple

2 And he said to them
    You see all this
    Certainly I say to you
    There will not be left here
    Stone upon stone
    Which shall not be thrown down

3 He sat on the Mount of Olives
And the disciples
Came to him on their own
    And said
      Tell us
      When will this happen
      And what will be the sign
      Of your advent
      And of the end of the age?

4 Jesus answered
    See that no one misleads you
5   As many will come in my name
    Saying
    I
    I am the Christ
    And many will lead you astray

6 When you hear of wars
    And reports of battles
    See that you are not disturbed
    As they must take place
    But that is not yet the end

7 For nation will rise against nation
And kingdom against kingdom
There will be famine and earthquakes
In many places

8 All this is the beginning
Of the pains of birth

9 They will hand you over to torture
And kill you
And you will be hated
By all nations
Because of my name

10 Then many will turn away
And will betray one another
And hate one another

11 Many false prophets will rise up
And will lead many astray

12 Because lawlessness will increase
Many people's love will grow cold

13 Whoever remains steadfast
To the end
Will be saved

14 This Gospel of the kingdom
Will be preached
In the whole inhabited world
As a witness to all nations
And then will come the end

15   Therefore when you see
The abomination of desolation
Of which the prophet Daniel spoke
Stand in the holy place
(Let the reader understand)

16   Then those in Judea
Should flee to the mountains

17   Anyone up on the roof
Should not come down
To take the things
Out of his house

18   Anyone out in the field
Should not turn back
To take his cloak
Which he left behind

19   Alas for the woman
In those days
With a child in her womb
Or one at her breast

20   Pray that your flight
May not be in winter
Or on a sabbath

21   As there will be great persecution
Such as there has not been
Since the beginning of the world
Until now
And could not be again

22   And if those days
        Were not cut short
        No-one living would be saved
        But for the sake of the elect
        Those days will be cut short

23   Then if anyone says to you
        See here is the Christ
        Or here
        Do not believe it

24   False Christs
        And false prophets
        Will rise up
        They will perform great signs
        And portents
        And if it were possible
        They would even mislead the elect

25   Now as you see
        I have already told you

The advent of the Son of Man
26   Therefore if they say to you
        See he is in the desert
        Do not go out
        See he is in the store-rooms
        Do not believe it

27   Just as the lightning
        Comes out of the east
        And shines as far as the west
        So will be the advent
        Of the Son of Man

28   Wherever the carcass is
        There the eagles will be gathered

29   Immediately
        After those days of persecution
        The sun
        Will be darkened
        And the moon
        Will not shed her beams

        The stars
        Will fall from heaven
        And the powers of the heavens
        Will be shaken

30   Then the sign of the Son of Man
        Will appear in heaven
        Then all the tribes of the earth
        Will mourn
        They will see the Son of Man
        Coming in the clouds of heaven
        With power and great glory
31   And he will send out his angels
        With a loud trumpet
        They will assemble the elect

Out of the four winds
From one end of the heavens
To the other

32   Learn this parable
From the fig tree
When the branch becomes tender
And puts out leaves
You are aware
That the summer is near

33   So you also
When you see all these things
Are aware that he is near
At the doors

34   Certainly I say to you
That this generation
Will by no means pass away
Before all this takes place
35   Heaven and earth
Will pass away
But my words
Will never pass away

36   Concerning that day
Or that hour
No one knows
Neither the angels of heaven
Nor the Son
But only the Father

37 As it was in the days of Noah
So will be the advent
Of the Son of Man

38 As it was in those days
Before the flood
When there was eating and drinking
Marrying and giving in marriage
Until the day when Noah
Went into the ark
39 And they were unaware
Until the flood came
And took them all

So will also be the advent
Of the Son of Man

40 Then two men
Will be out in the field
One will be taken
And one left

41 And of two women
Grinding at the mill
One will be taken
And one left

42 Watch therefore
Because you do not know
On what day
Your Lord is coming

43   But be aware of this
If the householder had known
In which part of the night
The thief was coming
He would have watched
And would not have allowed
That his house
Should be broken into

44   Therefore you
Must also be ready
Because the Son of Man
Will come at an hour
When you
Do not think of his coming

45   Who then is the trustworthy
And thoughtful servant
Whom the lord appointed
Over his household
To give to them the food
Which is due to them?

46   Blessed is that servant
Whom his lord
Will find doing this
When he comes

47   Certainly I say to you
That he will appoint him
Over all his property

48 But if the bad servant
Says in his heart
My lord is delayed

49 And begins to hit his fellow servants
And eats and drinks with drunkards

50 The lord of that servant
Will come
On a day
Which he did not expect
And in an hour
Of which he was not aware

51 He will cut him off
And his place
Will be among the hypocrites

There will be weeping
And gnashing of teeth

25 *Parable of the ten virgins*

1 Then the kingdom of the heavens
Will be like ten virgins
Who took their lamps with them
And went out
For a meeting with the bridegroom

2 Now five of them were foolish
And five thoughtful

3 Those who were foolish
Took their lamps with them

But did not take oil
4   The thoughtful
Took oil in their flasks
With their lamps

5   But the bridegroom delayed
And they all dropped off to sleep

6   In the middle of the night
There was a cry
Here is the bridegroom
Go out to meet him

7   Then all those virgins got up
And trimmed their lamps

8   So the foolish
Said to the thoughtful
Give us some of your oil
Because our lamps are going out

9   The thoughtful answered
There might not be enough
For us and for you
You should go rather
To those who sell oil
And buy some for yourselves

10   While they went away to buy it
The bridegroom came
Then those who were ready

Went into the marriage with him
And the door was shut

11 Later
Also the other virgins came and said
Lord
Lord
Open to us

12 But he answered
Certainly I say to you
I do not know you

13 Therefore keep watch
Because you do not know
Either the day or the hour

Parable of the talents

14 It is as if a man
Going out of the country
Called his own servants
And handed over to them
His property

15 To one he gave
Five talents weight of silver pieces
To another two
To another one
To each according to his ability
Then he left the country

16   At once
        He who had received five
        Talents of silver
        Went and traded with them
        And gained another five

17   So also
        He who had received two
        Gained another two

18   But he who had received one
        Went away
        And dug in the earth
        And hid his lord's silver

19   After a long time
        The lord of those servants
        Came to take their account

20   He who had received five talents
        Came to him
        Bringing another five
        And said
        Lord
        You handed over to me
        Five talents
        See how I have gained
        Five talents more

21   His lord said to him
        Well done
        Good and faithful servant
        You have been faithful
        Over a few things
        I will appoint you over many
        Enter into the joy of your lord

22   He who had received two talents
        Also came to him
        And said
        Lord
        You handed over to me
        Two talents
        See how I have gained
        Two talents more

23   His lord said to him
        Well done
        Good and faithful servant
        You have been faithful
        Over a few things
        I will appoint you over many
        Enter into the joy of your lord

24   Then he also came
        Who had received one talent
        And said
        Lord
        I was aware
        That you are a hard man

Reaping
Where you did not sow
And gathering
Where you did not scatter
25 And because I was afraid
I went away
And hid your talent in the earth
See here you have
What is your own

26 His lord answered him
Evil and idle servant
You know that I reap
Where I did not sow
And gather
From where I did not scatter

27 You should therefore
Have taken my silver pieces
To the bankers
So that when I came
I myself
Would have received what was mine
With interest

28 Therefore take the talent
Away from him
And give it to the one
Who has ten talents
29 For to everyone who has
More will be given

And he will have more than enough
But from him who has not
Even what he has
Will be taken away from him

30   And throw the useless servant
Into the outer darkness
There will be weeping
And gnashing of teeth

Prophecy of the sheep and the goats
31   When the Son of Man comes
Revealing his glory
And all the angels with him
He will sit on his glorious throne
32   And all the nations
Will gather before him

He will separate them
From one another
As the shepherd separates
The sheep from the goats
33   And will place the sheep
On his right
And the goats
On the left

34   The king
Will say to those on his right
Come
You who are blessed by my Father

Inherit the kingdom
Which has been made ready for you
From the foundation of the world

35   For I was hungry
And you gave me something to eat
I was thirsty
And you gave me a drink
I was a stranger
And you brought me in
36   Naked
And you clothed me
I was sick
And you visited me
I was in prison
And you came to me

37   Then the righteous will answer him
Lord
When did we see you hungry
And feed you
Or thirsty
And give you a drink?
38   When did we see you a stranger
And bring you in
Or naked
And clothe you?
39   And when did we see you
Sick or in prison and come to you?

40 And the king will answer them
Certainly I say to you
In so far
As you did it
To one of the least of my brothers
You did it to me

41 Then he will say
To those on the left
You who have been cursed
Go away from me
Into the fire
Which has been prepared
Throughout the ages
For the devil and his angels

42 For I was hungry
And you gave me nothing to eat
I was thirsty
And you did not give me a drink

43 A stranger
And you did not bring me in
Naked
And you did not clothe me
Sick and in prison
And you did not visit me

44 Then they will also answer
Lord
When did we see you
Hungry or thirsty

A stranger or naked
Sick or in prison
And did not help you?

45 He will answer them
Certainly I say to you
In as far
As you did not do it
To one of the least of these
Neither did you do it to me

46 And they will go away
Into punishment
Throughout the ages
But the righteous
Throughout the ages
Into life

26 *The anointing in Bethany*
1 It so happened
That when Jesus had ended his words
He said to the disciples
2 You know that after two days
It will be Passover
And the Son of Man
Will be handed over to be crucified

3 Then the Chief priests
And the elders of the people
Were gathered together
In the court of the high priest

Whose name was Caiaphas
4 And they considered
How they might take Jesus by stealth
And kill him

5 But they said
Not at the feast
As there might be a disturbance
Among the people

6 Now when Jesus was in Bethany
In the house of Simon the leper
7 A woman came to him
With an alabaster jar of ointment
Worth a great deal
And poured it on his head
As he sat at table

8 When they saw it
Some of the disciples were indignant
And said
Why this waste?
9 Could it not have been sold
For a high price
To be given to the poor?

10 As he was aware of this
Jesus said to them
Why do you trouble the woman?
For me she has performed
An honourable deed

11   You always have the poor with you
       But you do not always have me
12   She put this ointment on my body
       To do it for my burial

13   Certainly I say to you
       That wherever this Gospel is preached
       In all the world
       What she did will be related
       In memory of her

Judas betrays Jesus

14 Then one of the twelve
Called Judas Iscariot
Went to the chief priests
     And said
         What are you
         Willing to give to me
         If I myself
         Hand him over to you?

15 And they weighed him out
Thirty pieces of silver

16 From then on
He looked for the right moment
To betray him

Preparations for the Passover

17 On the first day of Unleavened Bread
The disciples came to Jesus

And said
> Where do you wish us to prepare
> For you to eat the Passover?

18 He said
> Go into the city
> To a certain person
> And say to him
> The Teacher says
> For me
> The moment is near
> I will keep the Passover
> With you
> With my disciples

19 The disciples
Did as Jesus had instructed them
And prepared the Passover

The Last Supper
20 When the evening came
He sat at table
With the twelve disciples

21 As they were eating
He said
> Certainly I say to you
> That one of you
> Will betray me

22   And filled with sadness
        Each one began to ask him
                Lord
                It is not I
                Myself?

23   He answered
                It is the one
                Who is dipping his hand
                Into the bowl with me
                Who will betray me

24   Indeed the Son of Man
                Is going
                As it has been written about him
                But woe to that man
                Through whom the Son of Man
                Is betrayed
                It would be better for that man
                If he had not been born

25   Judas
        Who was betraying him
        Answered
                Rabbi
                It is not I
                Myself?

        Jesus said to him
                That is what you say

26   As they were eating
Jesus took bread
And blessing it
He broke it
And gave it to the disciples
    And said
       Take and eat
       This is my body

27   He took a cup
And giving thanks
He gave it to them
    And said
       Drink from this
       All of you
28   For it is my blood
       Of the new covenant
       Which is poured out for many
       For the forgiveness of sins

29   Certainly I say to you
       From now on
       I will not drink
       Of this fruit of the vine
       Until that day
       When with you I drink it new
       In my Father's kingdom

30   When they had sung a hymn
They went out
To the Mount of Olives

Jesus foretells Peter's denial

31   Then Jesus said to them
          All of you
          Will turn away from me tonight
          As it has been written
          I will strike the shepherd
          And the sheep of the flock
          Will be scattered

32   But after I am raised up
          I will go before you
          To Galilee

33   Peter said to him
          If they all turn away from you
          Yet I
          I will never turn away

34   Jesus answered
          Certainly I say to you
          Tonight
          Before a cock crows
          You will disown me three times

35   Peter said to him
          Even if I must die with you
          By no means
          Will I disown you

      And all the disciples
      Said the same

Gethsemane

36 Jesus came with them
To a place called Gethsemane
   And said to the disciples
      Sit here
      While I go away and pray

37 So taking Peter
And the two sons of Zebedee
He began to be sorrowful and distressed

38   Then he said to them
         My living soul
         Is sorrowful unto death
         Stay here
         And watch with me

39 Going on a little further
He fell on his face
And prayed
   Saying
      My Father
      If it is possible
      Let this cup pass from me
      But not as I
      I will
      But you

40 When he came to the disciples
And found them sleeping
   He said to Peter

So you had not the strength
To watch with me
One hour

41   Watch and pray
That you do not come into temptation
Indeed the spirit is eager
But the flesh is weak

42   Again a second time
He went away and prayed
        Saying
            My Father
            If it is not possible
            For this to pass
            Unless I drink it
            May your will be done

43   He came back again
And found them sleeping
As their eyes were heavy

44   Again he left them
And went away
And prayed a third time
Saying the same words

45   Then he came to the disciples
        And said to them
            Sleep now and rest
            For see

The hour is near
When the Son of Man
Is to be betrayed
Into the hands of sinners

46   Get up now
And let us go
Look how near is my betrayer

47 Indeed
While he was still speaking
Judas came
One of the twelve
And a large crowd
With swords and clubs
Came with him
From the chief priests
And the elders of the people

48 The betrayer gave them a sign
        Saying
            Whoever I kiss
            He it is
            Take him

49 And at once
He came up to Jesus
        And said
            Greetings
            Rabbi
And kissed him warmly

50   But Jesus said to him
            Companion
            Why are you here?

Then they came up to Jesus
And laid hands on him
To take him away

51   But now
One of those who were with Jesus
Stretched out his hand
And drawing his sword
He struck the high priest's servant
And took off his ear

52   Then Jesus said to him
            Put your sword
            Back into its place
            For all who take the sword
            Will perish by the sword

53   Or do you think
            That I am not able
            To ask of my Father
            And he will bring to me now
            More than twelve legions of angels?
54   But then
            How are the Scriptures fulfilled
            That it must be so?

55   In that hour
Jesus said to the crowds
    Have you come out to take me
    With swords and clubs
    As if against a robber?
    Every day
    I sat teaching in the Temple
    And yet you did not arrest me

56   But all this has happened
    So that what the prophets wrote
    Might be fulfilled

Then all the disciples
Left him and fled

Jesus before Caiaphas
57   Then those who had taken Jesus
Led him away to Caiaphas
The high priest
Where the scribes and the elders
Had gathered together

58   Peter followed him at a distance
As far as the courtyard
Of the high priest
There he went inside
And sat with the attendants
To see the end

59   The chief priests
       And the whole council
       Tried to find false witnesses
       Against Jesus
       That they might put him to death

60   Although many false witnesses came
       They could not find anything

61   Finally there came two
              Who said
                     He declared
                     I am able to destroy
                     The shrine of God
                     And build it after three days

62   The high priest stood up
              And said to him
                     Do you answer nothing
                     To the evidence
                     That is given against you?

63   But Jesus was silent

              Then the high priest
              Said to him
                     I put you on oath
                     By the living God
                     That you tell us
                     If you are the Christ
                     The Son of God?

64   Jesus answered him
                That is what you say
                Yet I tell you
                That from now on
                You will see the Son of Man
                Sitting on the right of the Power
                And coming on the clouds of heaven

65 Then the high priest
    Rent apart his clothes
                And said
                        He has blasphemed
                        Do we need yet more witnesses?
                        For indeed you heard the blasphemy
                        How does it seem to you?

66   And they answered
                        He is liable
                        To be put to death

67 Then they spat in his face
    And ill-used him
                They also slapped him
68   Saying
                        Prophesy to us
                        Christ
                        Who was it
                        That hit you?

Peter's denial

69 Peter sat outside in the courtyard
And one of the maid-servants
    Came to him and said
        You too were with Jesus
        The Galilean

70 But he denied it
In front of them all
    And said
        I do not know
        What you are saying

71 Then he went out into the entrance
Where another maid saw him
    And said to those who were there
        He was with Jesus
        The Nazarene

72   Again he denied with an oath
        I do not know the man

73 After a little while
Those who were standing there
    Came to Peter and said
        It is true
        That you are one of them
        It is clear
        From the way you speak

74 Then he began to curse
And to swear
I do not know the man

And immediately
A cock crew

75 Then Peter
Remembered the words of Jesus
When he had said
Before a cock crows
You will disown me three times
And he went outside
And wept bitterly

27 *The death of Judas*
1 When dawn came
The chief priests
And the elders of the people
Considered how to proceed against Jesus
So as to put him to death

2 Then they tied him up
And led him away
To be handed over to Pilate
The governor

3 When Judas
Who had betrayed him
Saw that he had been condemned
He changed his mind

And gave the thirty pieces of silver
Back to the chief priests and elders
    And said
        I sinned
        I have betrayed innocent blood

4   But they answered
        Does that matter to us?
        Deal with that yourself

5 And he scattered the pieces of silver
In the shrine
And left

Then he went away
And hanged himself

6 But the chief priests
Took the silver pieces
    And said
        It is against the law
        To put them into the offertory
        As they are the price of blood

7 After due consideration
They bought the potter's field
In which to bury strangers
8 So to this day
That field is called
The Field of Blood

9 Then the words were fulfilled
Which were spoken
By the prophet Jeremiah
When he said
They took the thirty pieces of silver
The price
At which the one whom they valued
Had been priced by sons of Israel
10 *And gave them for the potter's field*
As the Lord directed me

Jesus before Pilate
11 Jesus
Stood in front of the governor
And the governor asked him
Are you
The King of the Jews?

Jesus said
You say so

12 He was accused
By the chief priests and the elders
But he did not answer

13 Then Pilate said to him
Do you not hear
What they witness against you?

14 To the governor's astonishment
He did not reply to anything

223

15 Now at a festival
The governor was accustomed
To release to the crowd
One prisoner whom they wanted

16 They had then a well-known prisoner
Called Barabbas

17 So when they were gathered together
Pilate said to them
Whom do you wish me
To release for you
Jesus Barabbas
Or Jesus called Christ?

18 He knew
That it was because of their jealousy
They had handed him over

19 As he sat in judgment
His wife sent to him
Saying
You must do nothing
To that just person
As today
I suffered a great deal
In a dream
Because of him

20 But the chief priests
And the elders
Convinced the crowds

That they should ask for Barabbas
And destroy Jesus

21   So the governor asked them
        Which of the two
        Do you wish me
        To release to you?

    And they said
        Barabbas

22   Pilate said to them
        Then what shall I do
        To Jesus called Christ?

    They all said
        Let him be crucified

23   But Pilate said
        Why
        What evil has he done?

    They cried out all the more
        Let him be crucified

24   When Pilate
Saw that there was nothing
To be gained
But rather
That there might be a disturbance
He took some water

And washed his hands
In front of the crowd
> Saying
>> I am innocent
>> Of the blood of this man
>> Deal with it yourselves

25   All the people answered
    His blood is on us
    And on our children

26 Then he released for them
Barabbas

Having had Jesus scourged
He handed him over
To be crucified

Jesus is mocked by the soldiers
27 The governor's soldiers
Took Jesus into the praetorium
And assembled the whole company
In his presence

28 They stripped him
And put a scarlet mantle on him

29 When they had plaited
A crown of thorns
They placed it on his head

226

And put a reed
In his right hand

Bending their knees
In front of him
They mocked him
    And said
        Hail
        King of the Jews

30   They spat at him
      And taking the reed
      They struck at his head

31   When they had mocked him
      They took the mantle off him
      And put on him his own clothes

      Then they led him away
      To be crucified

The Crucifixion
32   As they set out
      They came upon a man
      A Cyrenian
      Whose name was Simon
      And they pressed him into service
      To carry the cross

33   When they had come to a place
      Named Golgotha

Which is called
A place of a skull
34 They gave him wine to drink
Mixed with gall

Having tasted it
He did not wish to drink it

35 When he had been crucified
They threw dice
And divided his clothing

36 So sitting there
They kept a watch on him

37 Above his head
They put the accusation against him
On which was written
THIS IS JESUS
THE KING OF THE JEWS

38 Two bandits were crucified with him
One on the right
And one on the left

39 The people passing by
Blasphemed him
        Shaking their heads
40   And saying
                You
                Who would overthrow the shrine

> And build it in three days
> Save yourself
> If you are the Son of God
> Come down from the cross

41 In the same way
The chief priests
With the scribes and the elders
Also mocked him
> And said
42 > He saved others
> He cannot save himself
> He is King of Israel
> So let him now
> Come down from the cross
> And we will believe in him

43 > He trusted in God
> Who should deliver him now
> If he wishes to have him
> For he said
> I am God's Son

44 And the bandits crucified with him
Also reproached him

45 From the sixth hour
There was darkness over all the earth
Until the ninth hour

46   At about the ninth hour
      Jesus
      Called out in a loud voice
         Eli
         Eli
         Lama sabachthani
      Which is
      My God
      My God
      Why hast thou forsaken me?

47   Some of those standing there
   When they heard it
      Said
         He is calling Elijah

48   At once
   One of them ran
   And taking a sponge
   Filled it with vinegar
   Then put it on a reed
   And gave it to him to drink

49   But the rest said
         Leave him
         Let us see if Elijah
         Will come to save him

50   Again Jesus cried out
   In a loud voice
   And released his spirit

51 But now
The curtain of the shrine
Was rent in two
From top to bottom
The earth was shaken
And the rocks were split

52 The tombs were opened
And many bodies of the holy ones
Who had fallen asleep
Were raised
53 And coming out of the tombs
After he had risen
They entered the Holy City
And appeared to many

54 The centurion
And those who were with him
Guarding Jesus
Saw the earthquake
And everything that happened
And they were very much afraid
    And said
        It is true
        That this was a Son of God

55 There were many women
Watching from a distance
Who had followed him from Galilee
Serving him
56 Among them Mary Magdalene

And the mother
Of James and of Joseph
And the mother
Of the sons of Zebedee

The burial

57 When the evening came
A rich man from Arimathea
Whose name was Joseph
Himself a disciple of Jesus

58 Approached Pilate
And asked for the body of Jesus

Then Pilate ordered
That it should be given to him

59 Joseph took the body
And wrapped it
In a length of clean linen

60 Then placed it in his new tomb
Which he had hewn in the rock

When he had rolled a large stone
To the door of the tomb
He went away

61 Mary Magdalene
And the other Mary
Were sitting opposite the grave

A guard is set on the tomb

62 On the next day
That is
After the day of Preparation
The chief priests and the Pharisees
Assembled in the presence of Pilate

63   And said
         Sir
         We remember how that impostor
         Said while he was still alive
         After three days
         I will rise

64   Therefore
         Give orders that the grave
         Be secured until the third day
         As the disciples
         Might come and steal him
         And say to the people
         That he has been raised
         From the dead
         Then the last deception
         Will be worse than the first

65   Pilate said to them
         You have a watch
         Go and make it as secure
         As you know how

66   They went and made the grave secure
    Sealing the stone
    And setting a watch

28   *The Resurrection*

1   When the sabbath was over
    At daybreak
    On the first day after the sabbath
    Mary Magdalene
    And the other Mary
    Came to watch at the grave

2   But now
    There was a great earthquake
    As an angel of the Lord
    Descended out of heaven
    And coming close
    He rolled away the stone
    And sat upon it

3   His form was like lightning
    And his garment
    Was white as snow

4   And from fear of him
    The guards were shaken
    And became as if they were dead

5   But the angel
      Said to the women
        You should not be afraid

I know
That you are searching for Jesus
Who was crucified
He is not here
6   For he was raised
As he said

Come
Look at the place where he lay
7   And go quickly
To tell his disciples
That he was raised from the dead
Now he is going before you
To Galilee
There you will have sight of him
As I have told you

8   And going away quickly
From the tomb
With fear and great joy
They ran to give the news
To his disciples

9   And then Jesus met them
     And said
       Greetings

They came close
And holding his feet
They worshipped him

10 Then Jesus said to them
    Do not be afraid
    Go and give the news
    To my brothers
    So that they may go away
    Into Galilee
    And there
    They will have sight of me

The soldiers go to the chief priests

11 Now while they were going
Some of the watch
Went into the city
And told the chief priests
All that had happened

12 When they had met with the elders
And taken counsel
The chief priests
Gave enough silver to the soldiers
    And told them
13   You should say
    That during the night
    His disciples came
    And while we slept
    They stole him away

14   And if the governor hears of this
    We will convince him
    So that you need have no anxiety

15   They took the silver
    And did
    As they had been instructed

    And the story
    Has been spread about by the Jews
    Even to this day

Jesus sends the disciples out into the world

16   So the eleven disciples
    Went to Galilee
    To the mountain
    To which Jesus had sent them

17   When they saw him
    They worshipped him
    But some doubted

18   Jesus came up to them
    And spoke to them
    Saying
      All authority
      Has been given to me
      In heaven
      And on earth

19   Go therefore
    And make disciples of all the nations
    Baptizing them
    In the name of the Father

And of the Son
And of the Holy Spirit

20   Teaching them to obey everything
That I have commanded you
And how
I
I am with you
Every day
Until the ending of the age

References